How to save the world

How to save the world

STRATEGY FOR WORLD CONSERVATION

Robert Allen

Barnes and Noble Books
Totowa, New Jersey

IUCN   UNEP   WWF

This book is based on the World Conservation
Strategy prepared by the International Union for
Conservation of Nature and Natural Resources
(IUCN), with the advice, cooperation and
financial assistance of the United Nations
Environment Programme (UNEP) and the World
Wildlife Fund (WWF).

Illustrations: Patrick Virolle
Cartoons and cover design: Oliver Duke

First published in the USA 1980
by Barnes and Noble Books
81 Adams Drive, Totowa,
New Jersey 07512

ISBN 0-389-20011-5

Printed in Great Britain

Contents

Foreword

Sir Peter Scott
Chairman, World Wildlife Fund

The World Conservation Strategy, on which this book is based, represents several firsts in nature conservation. It is the first time that governments, non-governmental organizations and experts throughout the world have been involved in preparing a global conservation document. It is the first time that it has been clearly shown how conservation can contribute to the development objectives of governments, industry, commerce, organized labour and the professions. And it is the first time that development has been suggested as a major means of achieving conservation, instead of being viewed as an obstruction to it.

But, more important, it represents a change in attitude. The confident assertion of the 1950s and 1960s that man would find solutions to all his problems has been supplanted by a new humility, born of the realization that even man's most astonishing achievements cannot offset his disastrous devastation of the earth, its plants and its animals. What the Strategy says quite clearly is that only by working with nature can man survive; conservation is in the mainstream of human progress. We must recognize that we are a part of nature and must resolve that all our actions take this into account. Only on that basis can the fragile life-support systems of our planet be safeguarded and only thus can the development of our own species go forward.

Preface

David A Munro
Director General, IUCN

In early 1980 IUCN,[1] UNEP[2] and WWF[3] published the World Conservation Strategy in a pack format for decision makers. This paperback version of the Strategy, which has been written for the general reader, is based on the same information as that assembled and analysed for presentation in the pack, but it differs from the pack in style and layout and in providing both a fuller account of the importance of living resource conservation and a more detailed description of the priority conservation issues.

The notion of conservation of living resources — using them in such ways that vital stocks of plants and animals are maintained and their benefits enjoyed by succeeding generations — is not new, but many conservation battles remain to be fought and won. Conservation progress has been lamentably slow, largely because it has been seen as peripheral to mankind's continuing quest for social and economic welfare. The World Conservation Strategy shows that development — the satisfaction of human needs and the improvement of the quality of human life — depends upon conservation, and that conservation depends equally upon development. The Strategy aims to help advance the achievement of sustainable development through the conservation of living resources.

Many governments, non-governmental organizations and individuals from both developed and developing countries participated in the preparation of the Strategy. IUCN's membership of more than 450 government agencies and conservation organizations in over 100 countries were asked their views on conservation priorities. Two early drafts of the Strategy were sent for comment to IUCN members and to the 700 scientists and other experts who are members of IUCN's Commissions on ecology, threatened species, protected areas, environmental planning, environmental policy, law and administration, and environmental education. Their assistance is gratefully acknowledged.

The World Conservation Strategy was prepared by IUCN and commissioned by UNEP which, together with WWF, provided the financial support for its preparation and helped to develop its basic themes. The final draft of the Strategy was submitted to the Food and Agriculture Organization of the United Nations (FAO) and the United Nations Educational, Scientific and Cultural Organization (UNESCO) as well as to UNEP and WWF, and all four organizations reviewed it and made contributions to it. While this book is an unofficial version of the Strategy it owes as much to the support of these organizations as does the Strategy itself.

References

1. International Union for Conservation of Nature and Natural Resources, 1196 Gland, Switzerland
2. United Nations Environment Programme, Nairobi, Kenya
3. World Wildlife Fund, 1196 Gland, Switzerland

Chapter 1
Why the world needs saving now and how it can be done

Conservation or catastrophe?

Earth is the only place we know of in the universe that can support human life. Yet human activities are progressively making the planet less fit to live on. Current attempts by a quarter of the world's people to carry on consuming two-thirds of the world's resources and by half of the people simply to stay alive are destroying the very means by which all people can survive and prosper. Everywhere fertile soil is either built on or flushed into the sea; otherwise renewable resources are exploited beyond recovery, and pollutants are thrown like wrenches into the machinery of climate. As a result, the planet's capacity to support people is being irreversibly reduced at the very time when rising human numbers and consumption are making increasingly heavy demands on it.

A disappearing planet

The fertile soils of Himalayan valleys are being washed away in such quantities that a new island is forming in the Bay of Bengal,[1] an island of soil which, if the land had been properly managed, would still be growing food. Erosion is also rampant in developed countries. For example, in the century during which it has been cultivated, southern Iowa (USA) has lost as much as half its topsoil.[2]

If present rates of land impoverishment are allowed to persist, one-third of the world's cropland will disappear in a mere 20 years. The deserts are expanding at a rate of almost 60,000 square kilometres (23,000 square miles — an area twice the size of Belgium) a year. An area twice the size of Canada — 20 million square kilometres (nearly 8 million square miles) — is now on the brink of being turned into desert.[3]

Huge quantities of fertile soil are stripped from the land each year as a result of deforestation and poor land management:400 million tonnes a year from Colombia; 1000 million tonnes a year from Ethiopia;[4] 6000 million tonnes a year from India.[5] Even in the USA, with the largest soil conservation service in the world, so much soil has already gone that the country's potential to grow food has been cut by 10 to 15 per cent and perhaps by as much as 35 per cent.[6]

Fertile land is also disappearing under concrete and tarmac. Together, the USA and Canada submerge 4800 square kilometres (more than 1.2 million acres) of prime farmland under buildings, roads and reservoirs every year.[7]

In developing countries hundreds of millions of rural people are compelled by their poverty, and their consequent vulnerability to inflation, to destroy the means of their survival. In widening circles around their villages they strip trees and shrubs for fuel until the plants wither away and the villagers are forced to burn dung and stubble. The 400 million tonnes of dung and crop wastes that rural people burn annually are badly needed to regenerate soils already highly vulnerable to erosion now that the plants that bind them are disappearing.

Fuelwood is now so scarce in the Gambia that gathering it takes 360 woman days a year per household.[8] Even when firewood is available for sale, it is often beyond the budgets of poor householders. In the highlands of South Korea cooking and heating can cost up to 15 per cent of the household budget;[8] and in the poorer parts of the Andean Sierra and of Africa's Sahel it can be as high as 25 per cent.[9] Because of the cost many families are forced to do without.

Lack of soil and forest conservation contributes to the rising energy, financial and other costs of providing essential goods and services. Throughout the world, but especially in developing countries, siltation caused by deforestation and poor land management cuts the 'lifetimes' of reservoirs supplying water and hydroelectricity, often by as much as half. Large and increasing sums of money have to be spent on dredging docks and harbours to counter the effects of siltation. Floods devastate settlements and crops: in India the annual cost of floods ranges from $140 million to $750 million.[5, 10]

The resource base of major industries is shrinking as tropical forests rapidly contract and as the coastal support systems of fisheries are polluted or removed altogether. At present rates of clearance, the remaining area of unlogged productive forests will be halved by the end of this century.[11] It has been estimated that tropical rain forests (genetically the richest land environments on the planet) are being felled and burned at the rate of 11 million hectares (27 million acres) a year — about 20 hectares (50 acres) a minute.[12] At this rate *all* tropical rain forests will have disappeared within 85 years. Tropical forests are not uniform, however; nor is their rate of disappearance. The most valuable, and the richest in species, are lowland rain forests, and these are being destroyed at a much faster rate. Some, like the forests of west Africa and the lowland forests of Malaysia, Indonesia and the Philippines, seem unlikely to survive much beyond the turn of the century.

Overfishing has already deprived people of millions of tons of seafood. Now, as overfishing spreads, so too does destruction of the fisheries' support systems. Many coastal wetlands and shallows, the support systems of two-thirds of the world's fisheries, are either degraded already or are being destroyed by dredging, dumping, pollution or shore 'improvement'. In the USA the resulting losses to fisheries cost an estimated $86 million a year.[13]

As a result of the spread of environmental destruction, some 25,000 plant species[14] and more than 1000 species and subspecies of mammals, birds, amphibians, reptiles and fish[15] are threatened with extinction. These figures do not take account of the inevitable losses of small animal species, particularly of invertebrates like molluscs, insects and corals, whose habitats are being eliminated in their entirety. Indeed estimates that do attempt to take this factor into account suggest that from half a million to a million species will have been made extinct by the end of this century.[16]

Coming to terms with the facts of life

We have not yet learned to live with the one indispensable feature of our world: the biosphere, the thin covering of the planet that contains and sustains life. This failure has led to a virtually permanent reduction in the productive and regenerative capacities of the earth. We have reached a turning-point at which, depending on if and how we act, matters will be resolved for better or worse. We are confronted with a climacteric in the sense that human beings now have to live on a planet whose carrying capacity for all practical purposes is irreversibly less now than it was previously. Unless concerted action is taken immediately, there will be a further decline in the planet's capacity to support its population. Subsequent generations will be left a sorry heritage: less productive land; less diversity; less room for manoeuvre; fewer options; more people. The decision is not one we can postpone or ignore. Doing nothing is itself a decision to allow the world to be a much less fruitful and promising place than that into which we were born.

The decision to reverse the trend towards impoverishment of resources is not one that can be taken by some nations, communities and individuals, and not others. There is an unpleasant tendency by some groups in developed countries to assume that they will be untouched by the problems of developing countries and need not concern themselves with them. Similarly, some groups in developing countries are all too ready to take refuge in national sovereignty when their social and economic policies are criticized. Both attitudes may once have been appropriate when human impacts on the biosphere were local and when national economies were relatively self-sufficient. Now they are dangerously out-of-date. The components of the biosphere, including human communities, are interdependent. Today, although many human activities may have only local effects, many others have regional effects and some have global implications. There exist ecological, social and economic links that are often unsuspected or little understood, and too often are forgotten as soon as they are discovered.

The citizens of the industrial nations have been reminded forcibly of the fact of global energy interdependence by the two oil 'crises' of the 1970s. But what for them has meant inconvenience, added expense, and (in the USA particularly) exposure to violence from vehicular psychopaths in petrol queues, has been for the poor in developing countries the last straw. Many families and farmers have been forced to do without fuel and fertilizers; and some who once

14

burned kerosene are now obliged to burn wood, even though the areas from which they take the wood can ill afford the loss of vegetation.

For most people the destruction of vegetation in other countries is doubtless a remote affair with little meaning for them. Yet such apparently local actions can touch us all. Food production in the developed countries, for example, hangs by a thread to the genetic wealth of developing countries. More than 98 per cent of crop production in the USA is based on plant species brought in from outside.[17] As the genetic diversity of those crops is eroded by destruction of the vegetation in the areas where the crops originated, so the capacity of plant breeders to improve those crops and to protect them from pests and diseases will diminish.

The destruction of tropical forests, combined with the burning of fossil fuels, increases the amount of carbon dioxide being added to the global atmosphere. The likely result of these two sets of local actions is a global 'warming' which in turn could have profound effects on climate well beyond the tropics. Hence, as biologist Thomas E Lovejoy remarks, 'it is not absurd to adopt the view that the ability to harvest wheat in Kansas is linked to the success with which tropical rain forests are conserved.'[18]

Rural communities in developing countries are the most numerous victims of the biosphere's backlash against mankind's failure to conserve. But everybody contributes to the force of that backlash and everybody suffers, even if the urban citizens of developed countries so far have suffered only marginally and indirectly.

As the biosphere loses its elasticity — its capacity to recover from the effects of human pressure — and as everybody's demands on the biosphere increase, so choices will be harder and the room for manoeuvre will be reduced. If, for example, the USA or other developed countries wish to reduce their dependence on oil imports, they must among other things conserve their farmland and their soil. It has been estimated that in 1978 $1200 million of fertilizer would have been needed to replace the nutrients lost through soil erosion in that year.[19] The sum would be greater today and will continue to grow, not only because soil erosion is spreading but also because much fertilizer manufacture depends on oil. Now an estimated 50 million barrels of fuel equivalent are used every year to offset past US soil erosion losses.

The devastation of the biosphere is ultimately the greatest of all threats to the survival and well-being of human beings. It is seldom perceived as such because for many peoples and their governments it

15

is overshadowed by apparently more pressing concerns: war, poverty, epidemics, the energy crisis, inflation, unemployment. Nevertheless, failure to conserve living resources is closely linked to the worsening of the other problems. Continuing lack of conservation is likely to make life more expensive for the affluent and impossible for the poor. In so doing it will contribute to the rise in tension between the haves and the have-nots and hence to global instability.

The biopolitical facts of life are summed up in the striking image of our planet photographed from space, and in the slogan of the 1972 United Nations Conference on the Human Environment — 'Only One Earth'. Each carries the same message: for the first time in its history the human species must face the fact that it dwells on a single living planet. This message has two important implications: first, conservation of the biosphere is a prerequisite for human survival and well-being; second, interdependence is an inescapable fact of life. Progressively, the consequences of poor management of earth's living resources will be felt more quickly, more sharply, and more widely. To survive and flourish the self-styled *Homo sapiens* must be more ingenious in dealing with the biosphere and must become wise as well as clever. The human species has indeed reached a turning-point.

Conservation: how to have our cake and eat it

The biosphere is like a self-regenerating cake, and conservation is the conduct of our affairs so that we can have our cake and eat it too. As long as certain bits of the cake are not consumed and consumption of the rest of it is kept within certain limits, the cake will renew itself and provide for continuing consumption. For people to gain a decent livelihood from the earth without undermining its capacity to go on supporting them, they must conserve the biosphere. This means doing three things:

1. *Maintaining essential ecological processes and life-support systems.* Ecological processes and life-support systems are what make the living world tick. Essential ecological processes range from global phenomena such as the cycling of oxygen and carbon to local ones such as the pollination of flowers by insects or the dispersal of seeds by birds. In between these are many processes essential for human survival and well-being, notably soil formation and pro-

tection, the recycling of nutrients, and the cleansing of air and waters.

All of these processes are supported or strongly influenced by ecosystems — systems of plants, animals and micro-organisms together with non-living components of their environment such as forests and estuaries. The main ecosystems involved are the planet's life-support systems. These can be altered, sometimes greatly, provided the essential processes they support are not irreversibly impaired. The maintenance of these processes is vital for all societies, regardless of their stage of development. Many archaeological relics, whether of great civilizations or peasant villages, testify to the consequences of not doing so.

2. Preserving genetic diversity. Genetic diversity means the range of genetic variation present in the world's organisms: species, subspecies, varieties, strains and forms of plants, animals and micro-organisms. Some of this variation may be redundant, but (as we shall see in later chapters) a great deal is essential to sustain and improve food and fibre production through breeding programmes for crops, livestock, trees, forage plants and so on; to keep open future options; to provide a buffer against harmful environmental change; and to supply raw material for medical and scientific innovation, for pharmaceuticals, and for the many industries that use living resources.

The preservation of genetic diversity is a vital form of insurance and investment. It requires the prevention of the extinction of species and the preservation of as much of the variation within species as possible. Many species are highly variable, occurring in many different forms. The continuing availability of these different forms is of great importance to human welfare. This can be illustrated by two examples. The first concerns reserpine, a very effective drug in the treatment of hypertension. Reserpine comes from several species of serpentwood or *Rauvolfia*, plants growing in the tropical forests of Asia, Africa and the Americas, of which the most important today is African serpentwood. Most of the plants are collected from the wild, and it has been found that plants growing in one place may be much more effective than those growing elsewhere. For example, there is ten times more reserpine in serpentwood in Zaire than there is in neighbouring Uganda.[20]

The second example shows that a valuable variety may at first be overlooked because it lacks obviously desirable characters. A variety of wheat collected in Turkey was ignored for 15 years because it seemed so unpromising: it was thin-stemmed and collapsed in bad weather; it seldom survived the rigours of winter but it could not be persuaded to grow quickly enough for it to be planted late. Moreover, if it did survive to be harvested, its flour baked poorly. Suddenly stripe rust (a wheat disease) became serious in the USA and anxious farmers sought help. It was discovered that the apparently useless Turkish variety happened to be resistant to four kinds of stripe rust as well as to two other problem diseases. It is now used in all wheat breeding programmes in the north-western USA; and improved varieties based on it are saving millions of dollars every year in reduced losses to disease.[21]

3. *Utilizing species and ecosystems sustainably*. Sustainable utilization is a simple idea: we should utilize species and ecosystems at levels and in ways that allow them to go on renewing themselves for all practical purposes indefinitely. The main species groups and ecosystems concerned are fisheries, other wildlife that enters trade, forests and grazing lands. The importance of ensuring that utilization of an ecosystem or species is sustainable varies with a society's dependence on the resource in question. For a subsistence society, sustainable utilization of most, if not all, its living resources is essential. It is equally important for a society (whether developing or developed) with a 'one crop' or 'few crop' economy, depending largely on a particular living resource (for example, the fishing communities of eastern Canada). The greater the diversity and flexibility of the economy, the less the need to utilize certain resources sustainably, but by the same token the less the excuse not to.

Conservation is a matter both of respect for life and of making life easier by discovering and living by the rules of the biological game. But it is also something much more basic and urgent. Already for at least half of the world's population conservation is now a matter of life and death. People such as the peasant farmers, fishers, herders and hunters who make up about three-quarters of the populations of developing countries and people everywhere who suffer from diseases whose treatment depends on drugs of natural origin, are immediately vulnerable to resource impoverishment. The dependence of rural communities on nature and its resources is also direct and immediate. For the 500 million people who are malnourished,[22] or the 1500 million people whose only fuel is wood, dung or crop wastes,[8] or the 800 million people with incomes of $50 or less a year, conservation is the only thing between them and at best abject

18

misery,[23] at worst death. So it is for the millions of people suffering from hypertension, from several forms of cancer, or from other diseases that are relieved by drugs from plants, animals and other organisms. And ultimately, conservation is a life and death matter for everybody. The air we breathe and the soil in which we grow food are the products of living organisms. Without plants, animals and microbes, people would not exist.

How the world can be saved

No creature can be in a predicament more treacherous than the one in which human beings find themselves today. To survive, every species must modify its environment. But human societies are altering their environments so drastically — whether out of ignorance, greed, irresponsibility, or the desperate struggle to escape the trap of poverty — that they are making their survival unlikely if not impossible. It is as if the only means of improving our planetary home was to knock down the walls and bulldoze the foundations.

Although environmental modification is natural and a necessary part of development, this does not mean that all modification leads to development (nor that preservation impedes development). While it is inevitable that most of the planet will be modified by people and

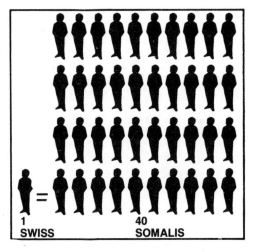

Disproportionate consumption of resources by the affluent. One Swiss consumes as much as 40 Somalis

19

that much of it will be transformed, it is not at all inevitable that such alterations will achieve the social and economic objectives of development. Unless it is based on conservation, much development will continue to have unacceptably harmful side-effects, provide reduced benefits or even fail altogether; and it will become impossible to meet the needs of today without foreclosing the achievement of tomorrow.

The way to save the world is to invent and apply patterns of development that also conserve the living resources essential for human survival and well-being. Living resource conservation is often thought of and treated as a specialized and somewhat limited activity, but in fact it is a process that cuts across and must be incorporated in all human activities. For this to be achieved, each of us will have radically to re-orientate our view of the world and of our place and role in it. Meanwhile, it is essential that conservation and development be fully integrated without delay to ensure that, in their quest for a higher quality of life, people protect those parts of the biosphere that need protecting and modify the rest only in ways that it can sustain. For this we need a world conservation strategy.

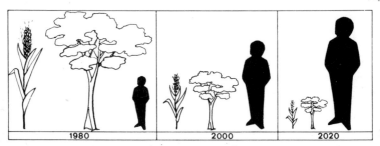

If current rates of land degradation continue, close to one-third of the world's arable land (symbolized by the stalk of grain) will be destroyed in the next 20 years. Similarly, by the end of this century (at present rates of clearance), the remaining area of unlogged productive tropical forest will be halved. During this period the world population is expected to increase by almost half — from just over 4000 million to just under 6000 million.

Why a world conservation strategy is needed

A world strategy for the conservation of the earth's living resources is needed for three reasons. First, the need for conservation is so pressing that it should be in the forefront of human endeavour. Yet for most people and their governments conservation is an obscure peripheral activity perpetrated by birdwatchers. One consequence of this view is that development, which should be the main means of solving human problems, is so little affected by conservation that too often it adds to human problems by destroying or degrading living resources essential for human welfare. A world strategy is needed to focus the attention of the world on conservation.

Second, national and international organizations concerned with conservation, whether governmental or non-governmental, are ill-organized and fragmented, split up among different interests such as agriculture, forestry, fisheries and wildlife. As a result there is duplication of effort, gaps in coverage, competition for money and influence, and conflict, when what is urgently needed is a concerted, cooperative effort. A world strategy is needed to promote that effort and define the areas where cooperation is most needed.

Third, the action required to cure the most serious current conservation problems and to prevent still worse ones takes time: time for planning, education, training, better organization and research. When such action is undertaken, it takes time for the biosphere to respond: reforestation, the restoration of degraded land, the recovery of depleted fisheries and so on are not instantaneous processes.

Time is running out. With every year that passes more essential resources are destroyed, while human demand for those resources increases. In the next 20 years the world population is expected to increase by almost half, from just over 4000 million to just under 6000 million.[24] Yet at present rates of destruction these people will have to make do with a third less farmland and only half the present area of productive tropical forest. Because remedial action takes so much time, it must be very well focused, concentrating only on the highest priorities, and it must be taken at once. A world strategy is needed to determine those priorities, indicate the main obstacles to achieving them, and propose ways of overcoming the obstacles. This is precisely what the world conservation strategy does.

Who needs the World Conservation Strategy?

Governments do. Although governments are generally aware of the need to conserve living resources, few take adequate account of conservation objectives when making policy or planning development. Few allocate or regulate use of their living resources to ensure

21

that the best sustainable uses are made of them. Many lack the financial or technical resources, the political will, or adequate legislative, institutional or public support for conservation (or any combination of these) to carry out fully the conservation measures required. The result is that the number of urgent conservation problems proliferates, while species decline and ecosystems are degraded. Few governments have the financial and technical resources to address all of the problems of living resource conservation at once. They therefore need to know what needs to be done first. Accordingly, the Strategy both recommends ways of overcoming the main obstacles to conservation and provides guidance on what action is most important.

Conservationists and others directly concerned with living resources need the Strategy in several ways:

— to remind users of living resources of the need for conservation;
— to remind those concerned with a particular living resource of the interdependence of living resources, of the need to ensure that conservation of the living resource concerned does not conflict with that of others, and of the advantages of cooperation with other conservationists;
— to indicate the main obstacles to living resource conservation and show how they can be overcome;
— to indicate those areas where conservation action is most urgently needed and where it is likely to yield the biggest and most lasting results;
— to propose ways for conservation to participate more effectively in the development process.

Specialists in agriculture and forestry, for example, need to be concerned as much with maintaining their resource base as with increasing production. They also need to work closely together since their concerns are often intimately related. Farmers need to ensure that the life-support systems of which their farms are part and the genetic diversity on which their crops depend are secured, and they have a role to play in achieving that security.

Wildlife conservationists specializing in particular groups of creatures — be they whales or butterflies, orchids or owls — have just as great an interest in seeing to it that the conservation climate is improved and that all countries' capacities for conservation are strengthened as in promoting their more specific concerns. All of these people and their organizations will continue to concentrate on their central objectives. The purpose of the Strategy is not to divert them from those objectives but to stimulate them into taking a broader, more integrated and cooperative approach to their achievement.

Similarly, for development practitioners the Strategy proposes ways of improving the prospects of sustainable development — development that is likely to achieve lasting satisfaction of human needs and improvement of the quality of human life — by integrating conservation into the development process. It also attempts to identify those areas where the interests of conservation and of development are most likely to coincide, and therefore where a closer partnership between the two processes would be particularly advantageous.

A brief guide to the World Conservation Strategy

The World Conservation Strategy is intended to stimulate a more focused approach to living resource conservation and to provide policy guidance on how this can be carried out. It concentrates on the main problems directly affecting the achievement of conservation's objectives: the maintenance of essential ecological processes and life-support systems, the preservation of genetic diversity, and the sustainable utilization of species and ecosystems. In particular, the Strategy identifies the action needed both to improve conservation efficiency and to integrate conservation and development.

Irrespective of its purpose, the function of every strategy is to:

— determine the priority requirements for achieving its
  objectives;
— identify the obstacles to meeting the requirements;
— propose the most cost-effective ways of overcoming those
  obstacles.

With resources limited and time running out, it is essential to be sure that the available resources and effort are applied to the highest priority requirements first, and only afterwards to lesser priorities. We are in exactly this situation with conservation, yet conservation organizations have seldom attempted to agree priorities. This is understandable, since there are so many urgent problems to be dealt with, people have different perceptions of priorities, and there have been few universally accepted criteria for what is important. However, it is precisely because there are so many requirements, most of them urgent, and many of them alone demanding all or more

23

of the resources at conservation's disposal, that priorities must be determined and followed. The first need, therefore, is for criteria for deciding priorities. There are three: significance, urgency, and irreversibility.

Significance is determined by asking such questions as:

— how important is this requirement in relation to the other requirements for achieving the objective concerned?
— what proportion of the global, regional, and national population depends on this requirement being met?
— how important is the requirement to the people most affected?
— how much of a particular resource will be conserved if the requirement is met?

Urgency is a function of the rate at which a significant problem will become worse if the requirement is not met and of the time required to meet that requirement.

Irreversibility is the key criterion: highest priority is given to significant, urgent requirements to prevent further irreversible damage to living resources, notably the extinction of species, the extinction of varieties of useful plants and animals, the loss of essential life-support systems, and severe soil degradation.

Priority problem areas

Using these criteria the problem areas of greatest and most immediate concern are outlined below.

Agricultural systems. In view of the scarcity of high-quality cropland, the rapidity with which it is being destroyed, and the rising demand for food and other agricultural products, it is vital that the most suitable land for crops be reserved for agriculture and that all cropland be managed to high standards. Loss of cropland and of soils and the disappearance of genetic resources essential for crop breeding have profound implications for everybody, since they presage the collapse of the biological basis of our food supply. The world's drylands, which cover about one-third of the earth's land surface, are particularly seriously affected. There the spread of desert conditions already jeopardizes the survival of almost 80 million people, and as many as 630 million could be threatened by it in coming years.[25] The problems of agricultural systems are the subject of Chapter 2.

Forests. Forest destruction means not only the loss of valuable products but also the decline of essential services, notably protection of watersheds (the upper parts of river basins). At least half the global population is affected by the way in which watershed areas are managed, for although only 10 per cent of the world's people live in mountain regions another 40 per cent live in the adjacent lowland basins.[8] The most endangered forests are tropical rain forests. The world has only about 10 years to save lowland tropical rain forests and no more than 20 years to save the rest. If it has not done so by then, not only will a huge store of vital genetic resources have been lost for ever but regional climates, and perhaps the global climate, could be changed for the worse. These problems, and measures to counteract them, are considered in Chapter 3.

The sea. The sea is so huge that it seems invulnerable to human impacts. Its most productive areas are close to shore, however, and are very heavily damaged by pollution, habitat destruction and overfishing. Coastal wetlands and shallows, together with the marine fisheries that depend on them, constitute the world's biggest wildlife resource. The mangroves and estuaries that support the fisheries are throughout the world either being polluted or destroyed altogether. Other marine areas are also strikingly important, particularly coral reefs, but are not yet under such universal pressure as coastal wetlands. Action to conserve them should be taken without delay to take advantage of the fact that they are not yet as badly off as temperate estuaries or tropical forests. These and other marine conservation issues are discussed in Chapter 4.

Endangered species. Thousands or possibly a million species and many more varieties are threatened with extinction, so it is difficult to know where to begin their conservation. In Chapter 5 the Strategy recommends concentrating on three types of threatened organism: those that are so different genetically from other species that their extinction would be an exceptionally great loss; those that are, or are closely related to, economically or culturally important species; and those that are so concentrated in certain areas that groups of them can be saved in one operation.

Priority actions

Three kinds of action are needed to ensure that conservation objectives will be achieved. The first is specific to the problem areas

25

and concerns the priority requirements for meeting the conservation needs of each. The second kind of action is much more fundamental since it aims to overcome the main obstacles to conservation irrespective of the problem area. The third strikes at underlying factors, such as population growth, over-consumption by the affluent, and poverty.

The priority requirements for achieving conservation with respect to each of the problem areas are discussed in detail in later chapters. Most are obvious: reserve good cropland for crops; manage cropland to high standards; protect watershed forests; protect the support systems of fisheries; control pollution; prevent the extinction of species; preserve as many varieties as possible of crop plants, forage plants, timber trees, livestock, animals for agriculture, microbes and other domesticated organisms and their wild relatives; establish comprehensive systems of protected areas; regulate international trade in wild plants and animals; reduce excessive catches to sustainable levels, and so on.

Obvious though they may be, these and similar requirements are often overlooked. One reason is that competition among different uses of land and water has become so acute that governments have become reluctant to take the actions conservationists recommend. Conservationists have given them little encouragement because often they have pushed for extreme courses of action, not recognizing the difficult trade-offs involved. Take, for example, the requirement to reserve good cropland for crops. On the face of it, it is straight-forward. The demand for food continues to grow but high quality cropland is scarce. Only one-tenth of the earth's land surface does not have a serious problem in agriculture.[9] Since it is not possible to relocate prime cropland but it is possible to be flexible about the siting of buildings and roads, agriculture should have precedence. However, the need for farmland competes not just with the need for building land but also with other conservation needs. Many wetlands are often essential nurseries and nutrient suppliers of fisheries, but when drained they make good cropland. Similarly, forest areas rich in species and ideal candidates as nature reserves might need to be cleared for crops or pasture. Governments need guidance on how to decide such difficult conflicts.

If the land is prime quality land, with no serious limitation for agriculture, then agriculture should still have priority, even over other conservation needs. If the land poses difficulties for farming, however, agriculture, while continuing to have priority over non-living resource uses (such as building), should be subordinated to the needs of genetic resource conservation and (in the case of wetlands) to those of fisheries.

The main reason for the failure to meet the priority conservation requirements, however, is the neglect of the second kind of action — action to overcome the main obstacles to conservation. Most nations are simply very poorly organized to conserve, lacking any system for building conservation into their decision-making process sufficiently early for conservation to be a positive influence on development rather than an irritant to it. Because these obstacles are the main block to progress, the World Conservation Strategy concentrates its attention on them.

Main obstacles

The obstacles to conservation are many and complex but the main ones are outlined below.

1. The belief that the conservation of living resources is a specialized activity rather than a process that cuts across and must be considered by all sectors of activity.
2. The consequent failure to integrate conservation with development.
3. A development process that is generally inflexible and needlessly destructive, because of inadequate environmental planning and a lack of rational allocation of land and water uses.
4. The lack of a capacity, because of inadequate legislation, to conserve; poor organization (notably government agencies with insufficient mandates and a lack of coordination); lack of trained personnel; and a lack of basic information on priorities, on the productive and regenerative capacities of the living resources concerned, and on the trade-offs between one management option and another.
5. The lack of support for conservation, because of a lack of awareness (other than at the most superficial level) of the need for conservation and of the responsibility to conserve amongst those who use or have an impact on living resources, including in many cases governments.
6. Failure to deliver conservation-based development where it is most needed, notably the rural areas of developing countries.

The need to tackle these obstacles must be kept constantly in mind. A species may be rescued, an area protected, or an environmental impact reduced, but such successes will be temporary or will be overshadowed by much greater failures unless every country's capacity to conserve is greatly improved and permanently strengthened.

Accordingly, the Strategy's recommendations for national action are devoted entirely to this set of issues. They begin with the proposal that every country (indeed every governing unit, such as the federal states in the USA and Canada's provinces, with responsibilities for planning and managing the use of living resources) should prepare a conservation strategy. Only in this way can wasteful *ad hoc* action and excessive concern for symptoms rather than causes be avoided. Details about national, regional and local conservation strategies and what they should aim to achieve are given in Chapter 6.

The Strategy goes on to establish priorities for international action. Although most action must be taken by and within countries, there are several aspects of conservation that can only be tackled internationally. Many living resources are shared by two or more nations. Many occur (temporarily or permanently) in areas beyond national jurisdiction, notably in the open ocean farther than 200 nautical miles from shore. Living resources in one state may be affected by activities carried out in another: for example, fish may be killed by acid rain originating with sulphur dioxide pollution in another country. These resources can be conserved only by international action. International action is also necessary to promote the conservation of resources (such as the genetic resources of crops) vital for the survival of all humanity, as well as to stimulate and support national action.

The Strategy therefore recommends a series of cooperative programmes concentrating on tropical forests and drylands, the establishment of protected areas for the preservation of genetic resources, the global commons (the open ocean, the atmospheric climate and Antarctica), and regional strategies for international river basins and seas. These programmes will provide an essential focus for international action in those areas in which it is indispensable, as well as for international support for national action to carry out other priorities of the Strategy.

Other strategies are needed too

Much habitat destruction and over-exploitation of living resources by individuals, communities and nations in the developing world is a response to relative poverty, caused or exacerbated by a combination of rising human numbers and inequities within and among nations. Peasant communities, for example, may be forced to cultivate steep, unstable slopes both because their growing numbers exceed the capacity of the land and because the fertile, easily managed valley bottoms have been taken over by large landowners. Similarly, many developing countries have so few natural resources and operate under such unfavourable conditions of international trade that often they have very little choice but to exploit forests, fisheries and other living resources unsustainably. In many parts of the world population pressures are making demands on resources beyond the capacity of those resources to sustain themselves. Every country should have a conscious and deliberate population policy to avoid as far as possible the development of such situations, and eventually to achieve a balance between numbers and environment. At the same time it is essential that the affluent constrain their demands on resources, and ideally reduce them, shifting some of their wealth to assisting the deprived. To a significant extent the survival and future of the poor depends on conservation and sharing by the rich.

These are some of the underlying factors which inhibit both conservation and development. It is beyond the scope of a conservation strategy to deal with all of them. Living resource conservation is just one of several conditions necessary to assure human survival and well-being, and a world conservation strategy is but one of a number of necessary strategies. Strategies for a new international economic order, for human rights, for overcoming poverty, and for population are also essential. The New International Development Strategy prepared by the United Nations deals with some of these issues. Strategies for the others are still urgently needed, for ultimately each is necessary for the others' success. Meanwhile, for the first time in history, a world strategy for living resource conservation now exists. It is long overdue.

References

1. Jayal, N D (1979) Ministry of Agriculture, New Delhi, personal communication

2. Diemel, R W (1979) A well kept secret. Agricultural Research, US Department of Agriculture, Washington DC

3. United Nations Conference on Desertification (1978) *Round-up, Plan of Action and Resolutions* United Nations, New York

4. Eckholm, Eric (1976) *Losing Ground: Environmental Stress and World Food Prospects* Norton

5. Das, D C (1977) Soil conservation practices and erosion control in India: a case study. *In Soil Conservation and Management in Developing Countries* FAO report of an expert consultation held in Rome, 22-6 November 1976 *FAO Soils Bulletin* **33**

6. Pimental, D *et al* (1976) Land depredation: effects on food and energy resources. *Science* **194**:149-53

7. Council on Environmental Quality (1975) *Environmental Quality: 6th Annual Report* Council on Environmental Quality, Washington DC

8. FAO (1978) Forestry for local community development. *FAO Forestry Paper* **7**

9. FAO (1978) *The State of Food and Agriculture 1977* Rome

10. Sterling, C (October 1976) Nepal. *Atlantic Monthly*

11. Lanly, J P and Clement, J (1979) *Present and Future Forest and Plantation Areas in the Tropics* FO: MISC 79/1. FAO Rome

12. Sommer, Adrian (1976) Attempt at an assessment of the world's tropical forests. *Unasylva* **28**:5-24

13. Kumpf, Herman E (1977) Economic impact of the effects of pollution on the coastal fisheries of the Atlantic and Gulf of Mexico regions of the United States of America. *FAO Fisheries Technical Paper* **172**. And Hester, Frank J (1976) Economic aspects of the effects of pollution on the marine and anadromous fisheries of the western United States of America. *FAO Fisheries Technical Paper* **162**

14. Lucas, Gren and Synge, Hugh (1978) *The IUCN Plant Red Data Book* IUCN, Gland

15. IUCN (1975) *Red Data Book* (separate, frequently revised volumes of fishes, amphibians and reptiles, birds and mammals) IUCN, Gland

16. Myers, Norma (1979) *The Sinking Ark* Pergamon

17. Schery, R W (1972) *Plants for Man* Prentice-Hall

18. Lovejoy, Thomas E, personal communication, 1978

19. US Comptroller General (1977) To protect tomorrow's food supply, soil conservation needs priority attention. Report to Congress, CED-77-30

20. Swain, Tony (1972) The significance of comparative phytochemistry in medical botany. In Tony Swain (ed): *Plants in the Development of Modern Medicine* Harvard University Press

21. Harlan, J R (1975) Seed crops. In O H Frankel and J G Hawkes (eds): *Crop Genetic Resources for Today and Tomorrow*. International Biological Programme **2** Cambridge University Press

22.FAO (1977) *The Fourth World Food Survey* FAO, Rome

23.World Bank (1978) *World Development Report*. World Bank, Washington DC

24.World Bank (1979) *World Development Report*. World Bank, Washington DC

25.United Nations Conference on Desertification (1977) *Desertification: An Overview* A/CONF 74/1, United Nations, New York

Chapter 2
Securing the food supply

The bottom is dropping out of the world's breadbasket. Prime farmland is being obliterated by roads and buildings. Cropland and grazing land are being mutilated on a huge scale by farming methods that more resemble mining than good husbandry. Wild and traditional crop varieties, the main weapons against pests and diseases that could wipe out harvest after harvest, are vanishing.

The problems

Loss of cropland

Prime farmland is a scarce resource that is getting scarcer. Only one-tenth of the world's land area is without problems for farming. The rest is either too dry or too wet, or has not enough soil, or the soil is either nutrient deficient, toxic, or permanently frozen. The limited amount of good land is distributed unevenly. Regions with the biggest proportion are Europe (36 per cent), central America (25 per cent), and North America (22 per cent). Those with the smallest are north and central Asia (10 per cent), south-east Asia (14 per cent), South America (15 per cent), and Australia (15 per cent).[1]

33

Much of this land, rare though it is, is being permanently taken out of agricultural use by being built upon. Between 1960 and 1971 Japan lost more than 7 per cent of its agricultural land to buildings and roads and European countries lost from 1.5 per cent (Norway) to almost 4.5 per cent (Netherlands).[2] Between 1961 and 1971 more than 8000 square kilometres (over 2 million acres) of Canada's prime farmland were lost through urbanization. For every increase of 1000 in Canada's urban population, 320 hectares (785 acres) of one of the world's main grain suppliers disappear.[3] During the last decade, the USA submerged more than 12,000 square kilometres (about 3 million acres) of agricultural land under concrete and tarmac every year.[4]

The impact of these losses will be felt by millions of people far away from the countries in which they are occurring. As Gus Speth, chairman of the US Council on Environmental Quality, says of the US losses: 'When you figure that we've got about 400 million acres (1.6 million square kilometres) under cultivation, and we're feeding about 300 million people, counting our exports, it means that every time we lose a couple million acres of cropland, that's a million people that aren't going to be fed.'[4] The impact will not just be confined to the food sector. In 1979 the USA earned $33,000 million from agricultural exports, enough to make up half the cost of the country's oil imports.[4]

Loss of soil

Not only is farmland disappearing at an alarming rate, but much that remains is being heavily degraded by bad farming practices. As much as one-third of the world's cropland will be destroyed in the next 20 years if current rates of land degradation continue.[5]

Soil is a crucial life-support system, since the bulk of all food production depends on it. Soil erosion is a natural and continuous process, but usually the soil is regenerated at the same rate as long as a sufficiently dense cover of vegetation remains. If soil and vegetation are not in balance, as often they are not when influenced by poorly managed human activities, erosion is accelerated with disastrous consequences. Even under natural conditions of vegetation cover, nature takes from 100 to 400 years or more to generate 10 millimetres (one-third of an inch) of topsoil;[6] and 2000 to 8500 years would be needed to generate soil to a depth of the length of this page. So once the soil has gone, for all practical purposes it has gone forever.

Soil loss has accelerated sharply throughout the food-hungry tropics which, because of topography and the nature of the soils and

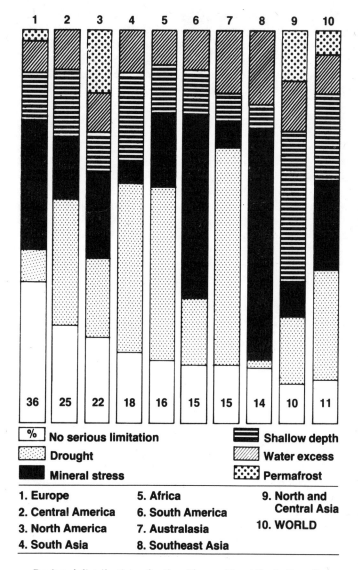

Regional distribution of soils with or without limitations for agriculture.

rainfall, are generally more susceptible to erosion than the temperate zone. More than half of India, for example, suffers from some form of soil degradation: of a total land area of 3.3 million square kilometres (800 million acres), 1.4 million square kilometres (340 million acres) are subject to erosion, and an additional 27,000 square kilometres (66 million acres) are being degraded by floods, salinity and alkalinity.[7] An estimated 6000 million tonnes of soil are lost every year from 800,000 square kilometres (almost 200 million acres) alone. With them are lost more than 6 million tonnes of nutrients, which is more than the amount applied as fertilizers.[8]

Excessive soil erosion is not, however, confined to the tropics. Even in the USA, with the world's largest soil conservation service, 12,000 square kilometres (3 million acres) of land are being degraded every year by soil loss, in addition to the 12,000 square kilometres that are being lost yearly to non-agricultural uses.[4]

Loss of the enemies of pests and the pollinators of crops

Agricultural productivity depends not only on maintaining soil quality but also on adopting cropping patterns and retaining a variety of habitats to encourage beneficial insects and other animals. These are important for the pollination of certain crops and for helping to suppress pests, as part of integrated programmes of pest control. Pests can no longer be controlled by heavy doses of pesticides, partly because of the rising cost of petroleum-derived products but largely because excessive pesticide use promotes resistance (the number of pesticide-resistant insects and mites has doubled in 12 years),[9] destroys natural enemies, turns formerly harmless species into pests, and contaminates food and feed. Instead pesticides should be used to supplement a battery of methods integrated in appropriate combinations.

These methods include the introduction of pest-resistant crop varieties, special planting combinations and patterns, mechanical methods, the use of repellents and hormones, and the encouragement of natural enemies.

Excessive pesticide use has often caused disastrous outbreaks of pests, which have then been overcome only with the aid of the pests' natural enemies. A dramatic example of this occurred 30 years ago in Peru, when in 1949 the organochlorine pesticides DDT, BHC and toxaphene were introduced into the cotton-growing area of Cañete Valley. At first the pesticides proved highly successful and yields went up from 494 kg per hectare (444 lbs per acre) in 1950 to 728 kg (654 lbs) in 1954. However, two years after applications began trouble started. By 1952, BHC had become ineffective against aphids, and in 1954 toxaphene could no longer control tobacco leafworm. Between 1955 and 1956, there was a population explosion of the moth *Heliothis virescens*, many of which were resistant to DDT, and at least six completely new pests appeared. That season, yields dropped to 332 kg per hectare (298 lbs per acre), even though the organochlorines had been replaced by organophosphate pesticides and the applications had been increased from once every two weeks to once every three days.

Clearly it is desirable for a permanent advantage over pests and diseases to be achieved. This is possible only when management practices are improved to take account of insect ecology. Thus in the Cañete Valley the blunderbuss onslaught on the enemies of crops has been abandoned with great success. Cotton production on marginal lands is now forbidden. The crop is no longer allowed to persist for more than a year, so fewer pests complete their life cycles. Bollworm pupae are killed by dry cultivation, optimal planting times have been established, and a fallowing period has been introduced. Beneficial insects have been reintroduced from neighbouring valleys, which fortunately had not been sprayed so this essential genetic reservoir had been conserved. Pesticides may be used only by special permission and are used minimally.

As a result, promoted pests (insects which become pests because the pesticides wipe out their predators) have been retired to their original innocence, and conventional pests have declined to tolerable levels. A year after these measures were first taken, cotton yields rose to 526 kg per hectare (472 lbs per acre), and since have fluctuated between 724 and 1036 kg per hectare (650 and 930 lbs per acre), the highest ever.

Some researchers are experimenting with ways of taking even more advantage of the wild enemies of crop pests. Scientists at the Philippines-based International Rice Research Institute, for example, have discovered that growing peanuts with maize reduces infestation by corn borer larvae (the main pest of maize) to one-sixth of the level found in maize alone. The principal predators of the corn borers are two species of wolf spider and many more of them were attracted into the crop with peanuts than that without.

Comparisons have been made between the effectiveness of the spiders and of various insecticides. Left untouched, the spiders did slightly better than a selective biological insecticide and three times

37

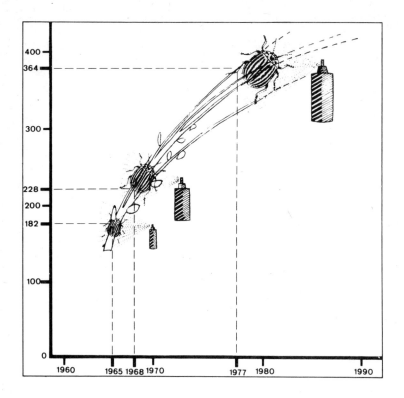

*Number of pesticide-resistant species
of insects and mites.*

better than regular applications of a broad-spectrum insecticide. The only way of improving on the spiders' performance was to apply insecticide at one specific point in the growing calendar and at no other time, and then the improvement was marginal.

Chemicals are a plant's principal weapon against its enemies, but they could not do without insect parasites and predators. Farmers and gardeners are obliged to intervene with artificial chemicals, when their planting patterns encourage abnormal pest populations. However, when possible, it is clearly preferable to adopt patterns that encourage parasites and predators, and if chemical applications still prove necessary, to ensure that they do not reduce their effectiveness.

Uncultivated land provides food, cover and breeding sites not only for pests and their predators but also for pollinators. Honey bees in the USA not only produce $125 million of honey a year, but also pollinate 50 kinds of crop worth a total of $2000 million a year.[10] In addition, wild bees and to a lesser extent other wild insects are important pollinators. Bumblebees, for example, are the main pollinators of blueberry, cranberry, clover, field bean and runner bean. Certain species of solitary bee are essential for the pollination of alfalfa (lucerne); and squash bees and figwasps, as their names suggest, are indispensable pollinators of squash and figs.[11]

Misuse of grazing land

Permanent pastures (land used for five years or more for herbaceous forage crops, whether cultivated or wild) are the most extensive land-use type in the world, occupying 30 million square kilometres (12 million square miles), or 20 per cent of the earth's land surface. Permanent pastures and other grazing land are usually unsuitable for crops without intensive capital investment. Their productivity is generally low, ranging from 1 hectare (2.45 acres) supporting three to five animal units on fertile, well-managed pastures in central Europe to 50-60 hectares (120-150 acres) to support one animal unit in Saudi Arabia. Nonetheless, grazing lands and forage support most of the world's 3000 million head of domesticated grazing animals, and hence most of the world's production of meat and milk.[1]

Unfortunately, mismanagement of grazing lands is widespread. Overstocking has severely degraded grazing lands in Africa's Sahelian and Sudanian zones and in parts of north Africa, the Mediterranean and the Near East, where it is a major contributor to the spread of deserts. In many of these areas farmers are moving on to land that is marginal for agriculture, thereby displacing pastoralists on to land that is marginal for livestock rearing. The results are poor and erratic harvests, emaciated animals and more desert. Overstocking together with uncontrolled grazing is also a serious problem in tropical and subtropical mountain areas, such as the Himalayas and the Andes. There too many improperly tended livestock remove both trees and grass cover (which is often very poor, both as forage and for soil protection) and erosion accelerates.

Loss of wild and traditional varieties

The genetic material contained in the domesticated varieties of crop plants, trees, livestock and aquatic animals, as well as in their wild relatives, is essential for the breeding programmes in which continued improvements in yields, nutritional quality, flavour, durability, pest and disease resistance, responsiveness to different soils and climates, and other qualities are achieved. These qualities are rarely, if ever, permanent. For example, the average lifetime of wheat and other cereal varieties in Europe and North America is only five to fifteen years. Pests and diseases evolve new strains and overcome resistance; climates alter; soils vary; consumer demands change. Farmers and other crop producers, therefore, cannot do without the reservoir of still-evolving possibilities available in the range of varieties of crop and domesticated animals, and their wild relatives.

The so-called 'green revolution', which is spearheading the constant struggle to reduce starvation and malnutrition, relies almost entirely on the breeding of improved crop varieties. For example, IR20, one of the new high-yield varieties of rice that perform well even when there is little fertilizer and the pests are being uncooperative, is a cross between one of the early high-yield strains (which yielded better in theory but were extremely susceptible to disease) and an obscure but hardy variety from southern India.

The continued existence of wild and primitive varieties of the world's crop plants is humanity's chief insurance against their destruction by the equivalents for those crops of chestnut blight and Dutch elm disease. This is not a remote eventuality. It happened once with the European grape vine. In the 1860s *Phylloxera*, an insect which lives on the roots of the vine, arrived in Europe from North America. Its effect was catastrophic. Almost every vineyard on the continent was destroyed. Then it was discovered that the native American vine is immune to *Phylloxera*. Europe's wine production was saved only by the grafting of European vines on to American rootstocks, a practice that continues today.[12]

The prospects of similar disasters striking other crops increase as farmers rely on fewer and fewer varieties. Because of intensive selection for uniformity and high performance, the genetic base of much modern food production has grown dangerously narrow. Only four varieties of wheat produce 75 per cent of the crop grown on the

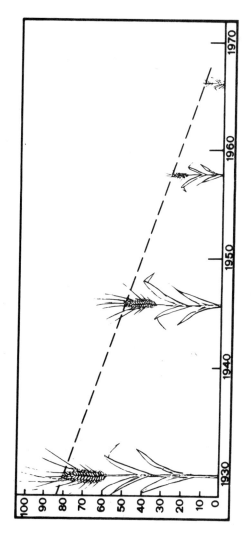

Loss of crop genetic diversity. Percentage of primitive cultivars in Greek wheat crop. The decline is typical of most crops in most countries.

Canadian prairies, and more than half the prairie wheatlands are devoted to a single variety (Neepawa).[13] Similarly, 72 per cent of US potato production depends on only four varieties, and just two varieties supply US pea production. Almost every coffee tree in Brazil descends from a single plant, and the entire US soybean industry is derived from a mere six plants from the same part of Asia.[14]

These and other crops in a similar position are extremely vulnerable to outbreaks of pests and diseases and to sudden unfavourable changes in growing conditions. Unfortunately, while the genetic base of the world's crops and other living resources is narrowing rapidly, the means by which this dangerous situation could be corrected (ie the diversity of crop varieties and relatives) are being destroyed. Many varieties of crop plants such as wheat, rice, maize, millet, beans, yams, tomatoes, potatoes, coconuts, bananas, limes and oranges have already disappeared forever and many more are in danger of following them.[15]

Valuable but primitive or locally distributed varieties are in large measure victims of their own utility, since the qualities of higher productivity and greater disease resistance that give the advanced varieties such as advantage over them are largely derived from them. The rapid replacement of traditional varieties by new ones is a necessary and positive development given the need for more food, but it could prove counter-productive if the traditional varieties and their wild relatives are not saved as well. Primitive populations of crops and their wild relatives are an important source, and often the only source, of pest and disease resistance worth many millions of dollars, of adaptations to difficult environments and of other agronomically valuable characteristics such as the dwarf habit in rice and wheat, which has revolutionized their cultivation and led to greatly increased yields in many parts of the world.

Useful breeds of livestock are also at risk. Of the 145 cattle breeds native to Europe and the Mediterranean region, 115 are threatened with extinction.[16] Yet, as with crops, many traditional strains are of great value for breeding. The Wensleydale sheep is a very local breed from Yorkshire, England, that became very rare. It was bypassed by modern and commercially more successful breeds such as the Dorset Horn and was almost forgotten. Now certain of its characteristics are of great value in breeding. It has a rapid rate of growth, produces wool of high quality, and, most interesting of all, is very tolerant of heat. For this reason it can be crossed with unimproved breeds of subtropical sheep. The very primitive breeds of sheep do not produce wool at all, having a hairy coat. Crossed with the Wensleydale the offspring is a heat-tolerant animal that produces good quality wool.[17]

The Cornish chicken is a classic example of how a breed with nothing but curiosity value can be transformed by science and new markets into a gold-mine. The Cornish hen is a quaint, somewhat ungainly animal, which until the 1940s was appreciated only by the Cornish and by poultry fanciers. It was promoted to international stardom by North American scientists who detected its usefulness for cross-breeding to produce a quick-growing meat bird. Today, most broiler chickens have a bit of Cornish hen in them.[18]

The case of the spreading deserts

Soil and vegetation are taking so heavy a beating from hooves and human implements that almost 38 million square kilometres (15 million square miles) — a quarter of the earth's land surface — is in danger of becoming desert. The creation of new desert areas is happening on a colossal scale. All over the world people are busy making life even more difficult than it already is. They are turning semi-desert into desert and desert into extreme desert, transforming the barely productive into the unproductively bare. The precious soil is either stripped from the land to fertilize the ocean or fill up reservoirs or it is sterilized by salt and alkali. Over much of the planet where two ears of corn or two blades of grass grew yesterday only one can grow today.[19]

The vulnerable areas are the drylands. Drylands, where rainfall is low and evaporation and transpiration are high, cover about a third of the earth's land surface. They are extremely prone to desertification (the process by which land becomes desert) unless used with care and skill, and they represent the most extensive ecological problem area on this planet.

It is estimated that almost 80 million people are immediately threatened by a desertification-induced drop in productivity of the land on which (directly or indirectly) they depend. Regions already in the grip of desertification or at high to very high risk cover 20 million square kilometres (9 million square miles), an area twice the size of Canada. The degree of risk is assessed on the basis of vulnerability of the land (a function of climate, terrain, soil and vegetation) combined with prevailing human or animal pressure. Very high risk means that the region will suffer very rapid desertification if present conditions do not change. Very high risk areas total more than 3 million square kilometres (1 million square miles), an area more than six times the size of France. Most of it is in Africa and Asia.

High risk means the region will suffer somewhat less rapid desertification if present conditions do not change. High risk areas total 16.5 million square kilometres (6.5 million square miles). Moderate risk means the region will undergo slow degradation if present conditions do not change. These regions total almost 18 million square kilometres (7 million square miles).

The total of moderate, high and very high risk areas plus the 8 million square kilometres (3 million square miles) that is naturally extreme desert constitutes 30 per cent of the earth's land surface. This huge area is either desert, becoming desert or in danger of becoming desert. No continent (except Antarctica, which is desert of a different kind) is spared. Desertification is a problem for as many as 63 countries. In 24 of them, all in Africa or Asia, all or virtually all of the land not already extreme desert is at risk.

The world's drylands, which by and large include the most important rangelands and wheat-growing areas, are being degraded at a rate of more than 58,000 square kilometres (23,000 square miles) a year, or 44 hectares (110 acres) a minute. Due to badly regulated irrigation, large areas are sterilized by salt and alkali. Over even larger areas, as a result of deforestation, overgrazing and poor farming practices, soil is stripped from the land to clog rivers and canals, fill up reservoirs and kill coral reefs.

Desertification occurs in patches: as if the earth's flesh were being plucked from its body by a giant flail. Few of the very high risk areas adjoin extreme desert, and more are in the semi-arid than the arid zone. This apparent paradox is symptomatic: pressure is greatest where conditions are marginally better. As the plant cover is destroyed so erosion increases, leaving eventually only the dry bones of the land — hard, sterile, unproductive. These bare patches link and spread, giving the impression that the deserts are advancing when in fact all too often they are taking us by surprise from behind. As ecologist H N Le Houérou points out 'it is man who creates the desert; the climate only provides the right conditions'.

Desertification is a function of the inherent vulnerability of the land and the pressure of human activities. Pressure of human numbers and numbers of livestock, together with unwise development projects, the extension of rain-fed agriculture into unsuitable areas, inadequate management of irrigated agriculture, overgrazing and overcollection of firewood, have already degraded or destroyed vast areas and caused great human suffering. These pressures continue. Farmers, for example, move into areas suitable only as pasture. In Niger farmers are now 100 kilometres (60 miles) north of their legal limit. In good years with high rainfall they can make a go of it, but in bad years they encounter severe problems.The soil, stripped of plant cover, is exposed to erosion by wind and water. Surfaces puddled by rain bake into a crust, increasing run-off. The precious topsoil disappears, blasting young crops on its wind-borne way and thus reducing still further the amount of plant cover.

Many drylands have soils and terrain that are highly productive when water is brought to them. Irrigation systems are important producers of cash crops. They allow the planting of trees, afford a consistent vegetation cover, raise the productivity of arid areas, and can prevent desertification. However, irrigation schemes are often costly and technically complex, demanding skilled management if unwelcome side-effects are to be avoided. These side-effects include waterlogging of soils (from seepage or overwatering), salinization and alkalinization. Only 4 per cent of the world's drylands are irrigated. Yet most of this land, perhaps as much as 80 per cent, suffers from some degree of salinization, and 25 per cent is affected by erosion. Each year as much land is lost because of faulty irrigation as is gained by new irrigation schemes.

Pastoralists, making do with less land as a result of its invasion by farmers or the desert, nevertheless maintain herds that would probably be too big even with the original amount of land. Many nomadic pastoralists are now being settled, chiefly around water holes and new wells with an imprudently generous watering capacity, and the surrounding area, trampled and overgrazed, soon turns to bare sand. More animals on less pasture, coupled with some sedentary ways, is a sure recipe for range destruction. In droughts the damage may be fatal. Whether in the rangelands of Australia and the United States or in the grazing pastures of Chile and north Africa, there is a natural reluctance to reduce livestock to match reduced pasture. And whether in rich lands or in poor, overgrazing plus drought is a deadly combination from which the land may never fully recover. Too little too late is the usual pattern, and does nothing to save the animals if the drought persists.

What should be done

Securing the food supply should be at the top of every government's agenda. Although many problems, such as soil loss and excessive use of pesticides, can be dealt with directly by farmers and other land users, the most important action required is to change government policy. Governments should do at least three things.

1. Give precedence to farming. Prime farmland is taken over by buildings and roads because towns tend to grow up in the middle of agricultural land and their expansion is poorly controlled, and because property values are much higher than agricultural values. Farmland near Washington DC, would sell for almost $40,000 per hectare ($15,000 per acre) to a suburban developer. But for a farmer to earn an equivalent return from that land, he would have to charge $12 for every bushel (35 litres) of corn, about four times the going rate.[4]

If conversion of land to non-agricultural users is left to the unregulated marketplace, the best farmland will continue to disappear quickly. Therefore, governments should first of all make a decision to give precedence to agriculture whenever there is competition between agriculture and other uses for high quality land. They can enforce that decision by prohibiting the sale of farmland, dropping government assistance for projects that would encourage conversion of farmland, and promoting the use of lower quality land as sites for urban development.

2. Start a top-level soil conservation service. Land users allow the land to degrade because they are after a quick buck, they do not know better, or they have no choice. With the costs of seeds, fertilizers, pesticides and equipment going up, with credit either short or expensive, and with market prices for produce uncertain, farmers are often tempted to wring more out of the land than it can sustain. They may neglect drainage, grow crops where grass alone is suitable, or convert to grass land that should remain wooded. Many farmers are simply unaware of the effects their actions this year will have on their capacity to grow food in future years. Or, if they are vaguely aware, they do not know what to do to make sure that any increase in productivity is sustainable. Millions of peasant farmers, especially in developing countries, are not in a position to conserve the soil, however knowledgeable they may be. Many are forced to cultivate steep, unstable slopes because their growing numbers exceed the capacity of the land and because the fertile, easily managed valley bottoms have been taken over by large landowners.

People need incentives to conserve. The best possible incentive for the farmer is demonstration that soil conservation brings big enough benefits, such as higher average yields for lower overall costs, quickly enough to make it worth the effort and expense. Every country, therefore, should have a soil conservation service with sufficient technical staff to help with as many demonstration projects as may be needed and professional staff to provide the technical workers with expert back-up.

If, however, it is clear that the benefits from conservation will be too gradual for the farmer alone to support the costs of conservation, other incentives, such as low-cost credit or tax concessions for installing and maintaining drains, retaining tree cover and recycling farm wastes, should be given. Land reform is often another indispensable incentive. People cannot be expected to look after land they do not own and from which they may be expelled without notice. 'Land to the tiller' is a cardinal maxim, and it must not just be the land the wealthy do not want.

The soil conservation service should not be just a technical, advisory body. It should also operate at the highest level of government, able to make and influence policy. There are two reasons for this. First, advice, education and exhortation, important though they are, can do little against a socio-political *status quo* promoting land degradation. A cheap food policy may be essential for the welfare of the urban poor but it is disastrous if it means low prices to the farmer. Second, farmers are not the only ones who degrade the land. So do foresters, road builders, miners and the construction industry. A soil conservation service will not be able to influence any of these people if it is buried in a particular ministry, like agriculture, and if it does not have the clout to alter the policies of a great many government departments.

3. Step up programmes to preserve crop and livestock genetic resources. The three ways of preserving the genetic diversity of the world's vanishing species and varieties are outlined below.

(a) On site — in which the stock is preserved by protecting the ecosystem in which it occurs naturally.

(b) Off site, part of the organism — in which the seed, semen or other element from which the organism concerned can be reproduced is preserved.

(c) Off site, whole animal — in which a stock of individuals of the organism concerned is kept outside their natural habitat in a plantation, botanical garden, zoo, aquarium or ranch.

All of these ways are necessary and each has advantages over the others. Off site preservation is generally cheaper and easier, except in the case of most wild animals and those wild plants whose seeds cannot be stored for long periods without deteriorating or which cannot be grown in monocultures.

It is not enough, however, to store the genetic material of plant and animal varieties in seed banks and the like (although such storage, where possible, is also essential). First, many crop plants cannot be stored in seed banks at all. Second, seed banks can fail because of accidents or carelessness: one of the largest collections of maize germ plasm in the world was lost from one bank when three refrigerator compressors broke down. Third, the characteristics of genetic materials kept in seed banks are frozen; plants and animals conserved in the wild can continue to evolve new strains to meet new demands.

The wild relatives and locally domesticated varieties of cultivated plants and domesticated animals must, therefore, also be preserved in the habitats in which they have evolved. The case for protecting such habitats is regularly strengthened by the discovery of new species related to staple crops. In 1977 scientists from Israel's Weizmann Institute discovered *Triticum searsii*, the only one of the three known progenitors of wheat that had not been found despite 60 years of searching. The species, which occurs in the area of the River Jordan watershed, is expected greatly to assist the breeding of new strains of wheat with high protein content and drought resistance.[20]

In 1978, high in the damp and sometimes snowy Sierra de Manantlan mountains of Mexico, Mexican and US scientists discovered a new species of maize. The species, *Zea diploperennis*, could help to expand food production because, unlike true maize, it flourishes in wet soil and at high altitudes (as high as 3000 metres) and does not need annual resowing. The latter is a particularly valuable attribute since much of the cost of growing corn is in ploughing under old crops and sowing new ones. Also, unlike its nearest relative, *Zea perennis*, it seems to produce fertile plants when cross-bred with true maize.[21]

Stopping desertification

In September 1977 the United Nations Conference on Desertification (UNCOD) agreed an impressive plan of action, largely directed at governments, to tackle desertification. The plan called for a wide range of activities to deal with the complex biological, social, economic and political factors involved, based on the development of proper land use, including conservation and enhancement of living resources and water resources. It envisaged the successful halting of desertification throughout the world by the end of this century through national programmes assisted by inter-governmental and non-governmental organizations coordinated by the United Nations Environment Programme (UNEP). The formidable cost, estimated at $15,625 million per year, was seen as coming from increased levels of international aid and assistance reinforced if possible by arrangements such as a special anti-desertification fund and an international taxation scheme.

Since then progress has been disappointingly slow. According to Professor Mohamed Kassas, President of the International Union for Conservation of Nature and Natural Resources (IUCN), neither the governments of the countries affected by desertification, nor the rich donor countries who were expected to provide substantial funds, have yet shown any serious commitment to the action that is desperately needed. Attempts to increase the flow of multilateral aid have stalled. The single exception is the Club du Sahel, a non-UN organization of governments, which has pledged more than $2000 million for the development of the Sahel countries.

Partly this may be due to lack of organization by countries suffering desertification. Each was supposed to set up an official focal point to coordinate its anti-desert activities. In many of the countries, however, the communications gap between government departments is so great that one might be preparing programmes to prevent desertification while another is setting up agricultural and pastoral projects that will increase it. Coordination is clearly vital, but not a single African government has set up a focal point. Partly, however, donor governments appear reluctant to give more money through UN organizations, even though recipient governments often prefer the absence of national strings that may go with multilateral aid.

The problem, therefore, is not one of not knowing what to do but of getting agreed action carried out. That action is obvious. For example, in countries where centuries of intensive human use have devastated the vegetation of large areas of dryland, there is much to rehabilitate but little left to preserve in the unexploited state. Emphasis should be on rehabilitation in areas with high human and animal population densities. Because of the high densities, the supply of alternative food, fuel, and employment, however difficult, is mandatory. In other countries, the emphasis should be on protecting some of the many remaining unexploited areas. Then there are still other countries which have both large areas of degraded dryland and large areas which have yet to be intensively exploited. Emphasis in these should be on both rehabilitation and protection.

References

1. FAO (1978) *The State of Food and Agriculture 1977* FAO, Rome

2. OECD (1979) *The State of the Environment: An Appraisal of Economic Conditions and Trends in OECD Countries.* ENV/Min (79), OECD, Paris

3. Geno, L M *Energy, Agriculture and the Environment.* Report to the Policy, Planning and Evolution Directorate, Planning and Finance, Environment Canada, Ottawa. Cited in Edward Goldsmith (1977) The future of an affluent society: the case of Canada. *Ecologist* 7:160-94

4. Thornton, Mary (November 1979) Food exports threatened by loss of farmland in US. *Washington Star*

5. United Nations Conference on Desertification (1978) *Round-up, Plan of Action and Resolutions* United Nations, New York

6. Constantinesco, I (1976) Soil conservation for developing countries. *FAO Soils Bulletin* **30**

7. Bali, Y P and Kanwar, J S (1977) Soil degradation in India. In Assessing soil degradation: FAO report of an FAO/UNEP consultation held in Rome, 18-20 January 1977. *FAO Soils Bulletin* **34**

8. Das, D C (1977) Soil conservation practices and erosion control in India: a case study. In Soil conservation and management in developing countries: FAO report of an expert consultation held in Rome, 22-6 November 1976. *FAO Soils Bulletin* **33**

9. FAO (1967) Report of first session of FAO working party on resistance of pests to pesticides. *FAO Meeting Report.* PL/1965/18, FAO 1968. Report of third session of FAO working party of experts on resistance of pests to pesticides. *FAO Meeting Report.* PL/1967/M/8, FAO 1977. Report of the first session of the FAO panel on pest resistance to pesticides and crop loss assessment. *FAO Plant Production and Protection Papers* **6**

10. Anon (18 June 1979) Bee's killer. *Time*

11. Free, J B (1970) *Insect Pollination of Crops.* Academic Press

12. Olmo, Harold P (1977) Introduction of disease and insect resistance in cultivated grapes. *California Agriculture* **31** (9):24-5

13. Cheshire, Bob (18 December 1978) Sowing the seeds of suspicion. *Maclean's*

14.Harlan, Jack R (1972) Genetic disaster. *Journal of Environmental Quality* **1**:212-15

15.Frankel, O H (ed) (1973) *Survey of Crop Genetic Resources in their Centres of Diversity: First Report* FAO/IBP. See also most issues of *Plant Genetic Resources Newsletter*

16.FAO/UNEP (1975) *Pilot Study on Conservation of Animal Genetic Resources*. FAO, Rome

17.Turner, Helen Newton (1977) Some aspects of sheep breeding in the tropics. In *Animal Breeding — Selected Articles from the World Animal Review. FAO Animal Production and Health Paper* **1**

18.UNEP (1976) *Overviews in the Priority Subject Areas, Oceans and Conservation of Nature, Wildlife and Genetic Resources* UNEP/Prog/4

19.These paragraphs are based on United Nations Conference on Desertification (1977) *Desertification: An Overview* A/CONF 74/1

20.Anon (November 1978) Wild wheat discovered, may help the hungry. *Wildlife*

21.Sullivan, Walter (5 February 1979) Hope of creating perennial corn raised by a new plant discovery. *New York Times*. And Anon (12 March 1979) Amazing maize. *Newsweek*

Chapter 3
Forests: saving the saviours

Environmental disasters, such as floods, droughts and outbreaks of pests, are invariably blamed on nature or on the deity. They are called natural disasters or acts of God, as if there was nothing people could do about them and no way they could have had any hand in their making. Yet nature is generally the great preventer and mitigator of disasters, and an increasing number of floods, droughts and similar afflictions have either been caused or exacerbated by the violence people do to natural areas.

Forests are the prime example of natural areas that contribute heavily to human welfare by acting as environmental buffers. Forests influence local and regional climates, generally by making them milder. They help to provide a continuous flow of clean water; some forests, notably tropical cloud forests, even increase the availability of water by intercepting moisture from clouds. Watershed forests are particularly important because they protect soil cover on site and protect areas downstream from floods and other harmful fluctuations in streamflow. Removal or degradation of watershed forests and pastures can cause great human suffering. Without the sponge-like effect of their vegetation, which retains moisture and releases it slowly, the flow of water becomes erratic, leading to both floods and water shortages. The increased rate of water run-off causes additional damage by stripping the soil away, depriving agriculture of nutrients while clogging reservoirs, irrigation systems, canals and docks with silt, and smothering coral reefs.

The problems

Yet watershed forests are being widely devastated by clearance for agriculture, logging and cutting for fuel, overgrazing, and badly managed road-building. The results can be extremely expensive. It costs Argentina $10 million a year to dredge silt from the estuary of the River Plate and keep Buenos Aires open to shipping. Yet 80 per cent of the 100 million tonnes of sediment that every year threaten to block the harbour comes from only 4 per cent of the drainage basin, the small but heavily overgrazed catchment area of the Bermejo River 1800 kilometres (1100 miles) upstream.[1]

Sedimentation

Sedimentation as a result of unwise or careless use of watershed forests can drastically reduce the economic life of reservoirs, hydroelectric facilities and irrigation systems. The capacity of India's Nizamsagar Reservoir has been more than halved, from almost 900 million cubic metres (1170 cubic yards) to less than 340 million cubic metres (440 cubic yards). Now there is not enough water to irrigate the 110,000 hectares (270,000 acres) of sugar-cane and rice for which it was intended, and hence not enough sugar-cane to supply local sugar factories.[2] Deforestation in northern Luzon in the Philippines has silted up the reservoir of the Ambuklao Dam so fast that its useful life has been reduced from 60 to 32 years.[3] Such problems are not confined to developing countries: it has been estimated, for example, that more than 1000 million cubic metres (1300 million cubic yards) of sediment are deposited every year in the major reservoirs of the USA.[4] Although they have not been calculated (indeed, probably cannot be), the global costs of sediment removal, river dredging, reconstruction of irrigation systems and loss of investment in expensive structures like dams must be huge.

Floods

Deforestation in India and Nepal was probably the major cause of the recent spate of disastrous floods in India and Bangladesh. Flooding costs India alone from \$140 million to \$750 million a year.[25] Typical of such disasters was the Alakamanda episode during the 1970 monsoon, when the Himalayan river of that name burst its banks. It was the start of a disastrous flood, without precedent in the river's history. Whole villages were carried away and enormous loads of silt were dumped downstream, ruining irrigation systems in the plains of Uttar Pradesh. 'Banks were eroded', writes journalist Sumi K Chauhan, 'and debris carried down the tributaries built up huge natural dams at the confluence with the main river. As the water pressure increased the dams collapsed, leading to flash floods.'[6] It was all the evidence local communities needed to demand an end to the extensive deforestation of the local watersheds.

Water shortages

Elsewhere in Asia, deforestation and poor land management have caused fluctuations in streamflows that have left high-yield varieties of rice with either too much or too little water, thereby reducing rather than raising yields. Deforestation and other unwise environmental manipulations (such as excessive channelization) probably also contributed to the severity of floods that in recent years have struck countries as diverse as the USA and the Philippines. Similarly, in Colombia, Norman Myers reports that 'several major cities...have to put up with electricity rationing as a consequence of widespread deforestation.'[7]

The biggest monument to the folly of poor watershed management, however, could well be the Panama Canal. The threat from deforestation is so great that Dr Frank Wadsworth, Director of the US Department of Agriculture's Institute of Tropical Forestry in Puerto Rico, claims that by the time Panama takes over its management from the United States, 'the Canal may have become a worthless ditch, a colossal monument to resource mismanagement.'[8]

Invasion by farmers has reduced the forest cover of the Panama Canal's watersheds from 85 per cent in 1952 to 35 per cent today. As a result, the bottom of Lake Alajuela is now 25 feet nearer the surface in some places, covered with a thick carpet of rich soil that has reduced its water capacity by 5 per cent. It is projected that by the year 2000 current land-use trends will reduce Lake Alajuela's capacity by 40 per cent. This would drastically affect power production and water supply, as well as reducing the passage of ships through the Canal. Already in 1977, some ships were forced to send part of their cargo across the isthmus by land, reloading it at the other coast, and certain bulk cargo shippers even abandoned the Canal, sending very large cargo carriers around Cape Horn.[8]

The diminishing store of goods and services

Besides protecting human communities from many forms of environmental harm, forests provide a huge variety of goods and services: timber, sawnwood and panels for construction, walls, doors, shuttering and furniture; pulpwood for pulp, paper, cartons and rayon; poles, posts, mining timbers and railway track sleepers; fuelwood, fodder, fruits, game meat, honey, pharmaceuticals, fibres, resins, gums, dyes, skins, waxes and oils; and products used for beauty care, amenity and recreation. Forests have unquestioned importance for industry and commerce. The value of the annual world production of forest products exceeds $115,500 million and international trade is worth about $40,000 million.[9] Thirty countries (eight of them developing countries) each earn more than $100 million a year from exports of forest products, and five of these each earn more than $1000 million a year.[10] Unfortunately, much of this exploitation is not sustainable. Without conservation, the real income from forest products may well decline.

In developing countries the heaviest demand on forests and woodlands is for fuel and as a site for a type of farming known as shifting cultivation. More than 1500 million people in developing countries depend on wood for cooking and keeping warm. Their annual consumption of wood is estimated to be more than 1000 million cubic metres (1300 million cubic yards), well over 80 per cent of the developing countries' total wood use (excluding exports).

In Africa the contribution of wood to total energy use is as high as 58 per cent; in south-east Asia and South America it is 42 per cent and 20 per cent respectively.[11]

The effect of such intense demand is to denude the land of wood over wide areas. Around one fishing centre in the Sahel region of Africa, where the drying of 40,000 tonnes of fish consumes 130,000 tonnes of wood every year, deforestation extends as far away as 100 kilometres (60 miles).[12]

A great many people still depend on forests to restore fertility to the soils that they farm. More than 200 million people occupying about 30 million square kilometres (12 million square miles) of

*Women in Mali carrying wood : because of the scarcity of fuelwood
many women days per year are devoted to this activity.*

tropical forests live by practising shifting cultivation, meaning that
they crop an area for a few years, then clear another area, leaving the
first one fallow to revert to scrub and forest. The fallow period lasts
from eight to 12 years in tropical rain forests to 20 to 30 years in drier
areas, and during this time the forest cover enables the soil to
regenerate. This is a stable, productive practice if the population
itself is stable. But if populations are growing, which they usually
are, the pressure on land increases, fallow periods shorten, the soil
has no chance to regenerate, and wider and wider swathes of
otherwise productive forest land are destroyed. Almost two-thirds of
the land under shifting cultivation is upland forest and the resulting
erosion is severe. In the Ivory Coast, shifting cultivation reduced the
forest cover by 30 per cent between 1956 and 1966 and now only 5
million hectares (12 million acres) remain of the 15 million hectares
(36 million acres) that it is believed existed at the beginning of this
century.[11]

The case of the vanishing rain forests

Our failure to apply rational ways of using forests is nowhere more apparent than in the rain forests of the tropics. Tropical rain forests are an invaluable renewable resource, acting as a reservoir of genetic diversity, yielding a continual supply of forest products if managed sustainably, helping to regenerate soils and protect them from erosion, protecting areas downstream from floods and siltation, buffering variations in climate and providing recreation and tourism. However, if tropical rain forests are exploited with scant regard for their characteristics, as generally they are, they cannot renew themselves.

Hence, as a result of expanding shifting cultivation, spontaneous settlement, planned colonization, clearance for plantations and cattle raising and excessive or badly managed logging, tropical rain forests are contracting rapidly. It has been estimated that tropical rain forests are being felled and burned at the rate of 110,000 square kilometres (43,000 square miles) a year. At this rate *all* of this forest type will have disappeared within 85 years,[13] and the lowland rain forests, the most valuable and the richest in species, are being destroyed at a much faster rate.

What makes tropical rain forests so special?

Tropical rain forests are the greatest, most enduring celebrations of life ever to have evolved on this planet. No other land environment has so many species of plant and animal. A hectare (2.45 acres) of temperate woodland, for example, normally contains an average of 10 different species of tree 10 centimetres (almost 4 inches) and upwards in diameter. Even the most diverse non-tropical forests, like those of the Appalachians or the 'cove' forests of South Carolina, contain no more than 25 species. By contrast, a hectare of tropical rain forest generally contains more than 100 species of large tree. Very rich areas, like the lowland forests of the Malay peninsula and Amazonia, boast more than 200 species.[14]

The profusion of plants and animals is remarkable. In the forests of south-east Asia, there are estimated to be more than 25,000 species of flowering plant, and 49 per cent of the genera (the main groups of species) represented are found nowhere else. Of the 660 different species of bird known or presumed to breed in the Malay peninsula, 444 are restricted to the rain forest.[15]

In a single hectare of Costa Rican forest, 269 bird species were observed, and in one locality in Peru, 410 were monitored. The total number of bird species found in the rain forests of central America is more than four times higher than that of the temperate forests of the eastern United States. Insects, amphibians and many other animals abound in equally impressive numbers.[16]

Some of the tropical rain forests are many millions of years old. Fossil deposits of pollen from the late Pliocene period have been found off the coast of Borneo and shown to be from the same genera of trees growing today in the Johore swamp forest of western Malaysia. So in some parts of south-east Asia, the forest has had a continuous history, on much the same site, since the flowering plants began.

As Professor Paul Richards has pointed out: 'The destruction in modern times of a forest that is millions of years old is a major event in the earth's history. It is larger in scale than the clearing of the forests of temperate Eurasia and America, and it will be accomplished in a much shorter time.'[17] In many cases, the plants that are doomed to disappear with the destruction of the forests of which they are part are undescribed or even undiscovered. The richest lowland areas are the most vulnerable. The plant communities of Malesian tropical rain forests (the Malesian floristic region embraces Malaysia, Indonesia, the Philippines and New Guinea) are the most species-rich in the world, but those of the Philippines and Malaysia are expected to have vanished completely within a decade. The loss will be irreparable.

Why does rain forest destruction matter?

It is currently estimated that about 50 per cent of the rainfall of the Amazon is generated by the forest itself.[18] Total removal of the Amazonian rain forest is unlikely to halve rainfall, but it is possible that at some point in the clearing process an irreversible drying trend would be set in motion, resulting in the automatic loss of the remaining forest and a severe impact on all activities within the basin.

Already the forests of Amazonia and south-east Asia are so reduced that local settlers and farmers are regularly suffering the twin experiences of floods and water shortages. The forests act as gigantic sponges, mopping up excess water and gradually releasing it, so that fluctuations in rainfall are ironed out. Now so much forest has been destroyed in parts of Indonesia, Malaysia and the Philippines that the farmers' new high-yield rice crops are running short of the water on which the high yields depend. Ironically, in one-third of the rice growing area of southern and south-east Asia, flood waters in the growing season are now commonly too deep for the short stems of the high-yield varieties.[7]

Destruction of tropical forests may have serious climatic effects well beyond the tropics. Tropical forests contain in their wood, leaves, litter and humus an enormous store (estimated to be 340 thousand million tonnes) of carbon.[19] Carbon is burned when fossil fuels are consumed or when forests are destroyed and it accumulates in the atmosphere. The latest estimates suggest that tropical forest destruction is now so intense that it is releasing as much carbon dioxide as comes from the use of fossil fuels. The likely consequence of the accumulation of carbon dioxide in the atmosphere is that the global climate will become warmer, and that the warming will be greater at the poles than between them.[20] Nobody knows the effects of this uneven warming, but it is quite possible that one of the effects would be a general drying in the wheat growing areas of North America. Another possible effect is an increase in sea level if the western ice sheet in Antarctica were to melt, as it did in earlier geological times during a similar warm period.

The world is wedded to tropical forests and their fate not only because of their influence on climate, but in more immediate ways as well. Products that directly or indirectly come from rain forests are ubiquitous: in hospitals, shops and homes, and on the road. Without them, many industries would find their costs rising and some might collapse altogether. A number of simple daily pleasures could become things of the past.

Every time we drink coffee, eat chocolate, bananas or nuts, or use anything made of natural rubber, we are enjoying the tropical rain forests. Brazil nuts, cashew nuts, passion fruit, papaya, avocados, cacao and bananas are all plants of the rain forests. If Africa's forests go, so will all the wild banana varieties. If South and central America's forests go, so will all the wild varieties of cocoa, rubber, avocado and cashew nuts, as well as Brazil nuts which are collected from the wild. The plantations will be left almost totally exposed to the unconquerable pest or disease that may emerge.

Tropical forests are often portrayed as dangerous, but many of their products are used in medical treatment. Major surgery depends on curare or some similar substance to paralyse the nerves. Curare, an invention of Amerindian tribes, is made from plants found only in the tropical forests of South America. Another important surgical drug, eserine, comes from the calabar bean growing in the tropical forests of west Africa. And if the operation is on the heart, serpentroot from south-east Asia's tropical rain forests will be used to keep it going.

Rauvolfia is a blessing to a great many people. One of its active constituents, ajmaline, is used to promote a regular heartbeat. Another, reserpine, relieves hypertension. For 4000 years serpentroot has been used in Hindu medicine to treat snake-bites, dysentery, cholera, fever and nervous disorders. In the late 1940s western medicine discovered that the plant relieved hypertension and schizophrenia, and by the mid-1950s reserpine had become the main source material for tranquillizers.

Before these discoveries high blood pressure made a patient very vulnerable to a stroke, heart failure or kidney failure, but today a large proportion of such cases can be helped. Because of this one plant, still taken from the wild, many millions of people are able to lead a relatively normal and healthy life, freed at least partially from hypertension (the greatest and fastest-growing cause of death in industrialized societies).[21]

The destruction of tropical rain forests will wipe out thousands of species. It is estimated that as many as half of the world's land species live only in the rain forests of the tropics. For example, some 660 species of birds are known or presumed to breed in the Malesian floristic region. Of these, 70 per cent are birds of the inland forest and only 18 of these species live in open country as well as forest. In Malaya itself, 65 per cent of the breeding birds are confined to inland forest. Similarly 53 per cent of Malaya's ground dwelling mammals are restricted to primary lowland rain forest, and most (183 species) of the frogs and other amphibians in Borneo are confined to primary forest.[22]

Tropical rain forests are not uniform. They vary greatly from continent to continent, and there are also striking local differences within each continental bloc. The magnificent dipterocarp trees are very largely confined to south-east Asia (about 500 species), with only a handful in Africa and none in America. By contrast, the epiphytic Bromeliads (plants of the pineapple family, growing on other plants but not dependent on them for nutrients) are virtually restricted to the Americas (between 1800 and 2000 species) with only one species in Africa and none in Asia.

Among the birds, tree hoopoes are confined to the forests of Africa, trumpeters to north-east South America, and the gardening bower birds to the montane forests of New Guinea. Local variations, which are just as sharp, reflect differences in altitude, humidity and soil, as well as factors we do not yet understand. Even where soils and climate are similar, there is an inexplicably patchy distribution of both plant and animal species. Thus it is possible to destroy an area of rain forest under the illusion that there is plenty more where it came from, and, in so doing, to eliminate for all time a priceless part of a national and global heritage.

What are the problems?

Tropical rain forests are succumbing chiefly to the combined pressures of shifting cultivation, planned colonization, timber exploitation and ranching. These activities in themselves are necessary and benign, but when pursued carelessly, in ignorance or in greed, they can be disastrous. Unfortunately, the instruments of change are often blunt, and they are wielded in ways quite insensitive to the special nature of the rain forest environment.

Government departments, plantation and ranch owners, civil engineers and lumbermen today have at their command vast machines that can quickly reduce forest giants to shavings. Monster caterpillar tractors with cable winch and blade slice through trees at the base like a razor through skin. 'Tree-pullers' exert tractor power at heights, 'tree-stingers' ram the stubborn ones, and the 'tree-crusher' can topple and pulp the greatest tree in a few minutes. With machines such as these, a hectare (2.45 acres) of tropical forest — 900 tonnes of living plants — can be cleared in only two hours.

Unfortunately, with the exception of recent alluvial and rich volcanic soils, tropical rain forest soils are generally very poor. In the Amazon drainage of Colombia, for example, the soils have low fertility, high acidity, virtually no calcium, magnesium or potassium in a form that can be taken up by plants, scarcely any phosphorus, and an excess of aluminium.[23] The forest flourishes in such highly unpromising circumstances because it is extremely thrifty in its uptake of nutrients and because it recycles them very quickly and thoroughly.

Most of the nutrients are stored in living vegetation. Those in dead and discarded plant and animal matter are taken up almost immediately by the roots of living plants and transported by the numerous fungal hyphae (the fungal equivalent of roots) in the litter and surface soil. The process is extremely efficient, and almost nothing escapes. Near Manaus (Brazil), for example, litter falling to the forest floor contains about 18 kilograms of calcium per hectare (16 pounds per acre) yet the concentration in local streams is too small to be detected. This efficiency is probably an adaptation to the high rainfall, which is seldom fewer than 2000 millimetres (78 inches) and in some areas (such as the Choco district of Colombia) more than

7500 millimetres (290 inches).[23] In such conditions, it is unwise to leave nutrients lying around, and the tropical rain forest has responded appropriately by evolving a virtually leak-proof system.

According to the Food and Agriculture Organization of the United Nations (FAO), between five and 10 million hectares (12 and 24 million acres) of forest are being felled each year for agriculture alone.[24] Some of this is spontaneous, reflecting the flight of peasants from land that has been over-exploited elsewhere, and from an oppressively feudal system of land tenure. They go where the roads go. Whatever their original purpose (to link cities, and to serve new oil or gas fields, mining developments, or logging operations), roads attract the landless and adventurous, who, unfamiliar with the peculiar characteristics of the forest, widen the swathe of destruction still further.

Often settlement is organized by government. At times, this is for the very best of motives, even though the results are unfortunate and could be avoided. In western Malaysia, the lowland dipterocarp forests are being felled to provide land for the landless under large-scale cooperative settlement schemes designed to produce cash crops like rubber. At other times the motives are more obscure. A distorted version of nationalism apparently demands that remote uninhabited areas be dragged into the country's economy before they are needed, or before it is known how best to use them.

Badly organized timber operations are degrading the forests as effectively as expansionist agricultural and settlement schemes. In a given forest section, only a few species (from 15 to 25 trees per hectare in rich and accessible areas, but often as few as two per hectare elsewhere) may be considered of commercial value. Yet to reach them, 75 per cent of the surrounding canopy is destroyed. The *apparently* endless supply discourages caution.

The volume of wood harvested is increasing rapidly. Thus, Indonesia's timber exports rose from 301,000 cubic metres (390,000 cubic yards) in 1966 to 7,413,000 cubic metres (9,634,000 cubic yards) in 1970. During the next 20 years world demand for tropical hardwood log production is expected to triple, requiring the cutting of 556 million hectares (1360 million acres) of forest.[25]

Although some lumber companies behave responsibly, many exploit the forest, heedless of the consequences for the nation they are working in and concerned only for their own profits. Such companies, damaging seedlings and saplings, disrupt the mix of tree species and sometimes expose soil to erosion over large areas.

A recent study in Sabah (Malaysian Borneo) showed that almost 70 per cent of the trees retained were damaged during selective logging of the forest.[26] In Indonesia, 27 million hectares (66 million acres) are officially classified as denuded by uncontrolled cutting, and the country still has too few trained foresters to supervise the enormous expansion of timber production. Thus the government relies almost entirely on the good faith of the companies.[27]

Japanese companies have been offering investments of $80 million to $500 million to log the Amazon rain forests. It is very difficult for hard-pressed, ambitious governments to resist such beguiling inducements, even though the result will be the destruction of a resource which, carefully used, could have lasted indefinitely. Ill-conceived farming and logging schemes have been succinctly condemned by the Brazilian Amaro Theodoro Damasceno as 'destroying gold for the production of silver', but governments and development agencies have persisted in viewing only the silver as negotiable.[28]

In many parts of South America the gold of the rain forests is turned not into silver but into dross. Large tracts of forest are being burned down and converted into ranchland. There beef is raised cheaply enough to satisfy demand in the United States, Canada and Europe, but it is a destructive business: the pasture is invaded by scrub so rapidly that after a few years it becomes uneconomic to maintain and is abandoned.

We are at the point where what goes now is gone forever. Once destruction is widespread, tropical rain forests can no longer be reconstructed. Recolonization from remaining stands can take place only if those stands are sufficiently large and close enough together. The forest's innumerable plant species are widely dispersed. Most of them depend for their regeneration not on physical agents such as wind or water but on animals: insects, birds and bats to pollinate the flowers; other animals to disperse the seeds and help them germinate. The mighty jungles, the parents of the planet's vegetation, are the children of plants that no longer exist. The magnificent progress from bare rock to high forest cannot be repeated.

What should be done

Forests, particularly tropical forests, are succumbing to two sets of very different pressures. One is the result of poverty combined with population growth — the desperate struggle of peasant forest-dwellers to stay alive and earn a decent livelihood. The other is the

64

result of excessive or carelessly applied commercial demand, largely by people in developed countries.

To save the forests from the first set of pressures, we must greatly accelerate rural development. Development must be based on conservation, however, if it is not to destroy forests just as thoroughly as does the current lack of development. Conservation-based rural development is described in Chapter 6. In the case of forest destruction by excessive firewood collection it would include such actions as the establishment of plantations for firewood large enough to meet higher levels of demand than today's; the provision of alternative sources of firewood to take pressure off the plantations and remaining vegetation; the restoration of the vegetation; and the provision of stoves that use firewood more efficiently and alternative sources of energy such as biogas (methane) and solar energy.

Dealing with the second set of pressures requires insisting that all forest exploitation is managed to high standards. The siting and management of timber operations should be such that essential processes (especially watershed protection) are maintained. Unnecessary damage to trees that are not used should be avoided. Felling programmes should be matched by planting programmes, as far as possible using the species exploited, so that what is taken out is replaced. Most timber companies are capable of taking all the necessary measures and should undertake to do so, but governments should make sure that they are capable of inspecting and controlling the conduct of commercial logging operations before they start.

It is not enough, however, to ensure that commercial logging operations are conducted with care. Demand levels must also be reduced. Many forests, particularly lowland rain forests, simply cannot withstand current demand, whether it be for wood products or for farming land. Developing countries need financial and technical help to get them out of the trap of needing to mine otherwise renewable resources to earn foreign exchange. Developed countries and citizens need to be educated to act with greater restraint, if necessary through international measures to raise the price of forest (especially rain forest) products. The prospect of this kind of action is, of course, remote, but it is necessary.

Uncontrolled logging often paves the way for uncontrolled settlement. Governments must control both if there is any likelihood that spontaneous settlement will occur in a forest area once it has been opened up for logging. Governments should also ensure that they have a practicable plan for assisting settlers to develop the land sustainably, providing firewood plantations or alternative fuels, securing essential processes, and protecting important genetic resources.

International action to conserve tropical forests

International action is needed to help developing countries to conserve their forests. The priority regions for international action clearly must be those where destruction is most advanced: west and east Africa, south and south-east central America and Mexico, and parts of South America. In west and east Africa the most urgent needs are:

1. Establishment of fuelwood plantations (present ones are quite insufficient).
2. Establishment of industrial plantations (existing and planned plantations will not even approach compensating the region for the projected loss of its natural forest resources).
3. In those countries that have established national parks or nature reserves to protect genetic resources, strengthening of such parks or reserves, in particular by allowing local people to benefit from buffer zones and by making surrounding areas priorities for rural development.
4. In those countries that have not established such parks or reserves, or where they are insufficient, identification of areas of greatest genetic importance and where pressure is least, and establishment of parks and reserves in those areas.
5. Strengthening of administrations responsible for protection and management of the natural forest resource.
6. Reafforestation including well-designed and strategically located managed production forests, designated to meet not only immediate needs for raw materials and to serve as model examples for the development of neighbouring areas, but also to replace areas of forest already destroyed.

Madagascar, Ethiopia, east Africa's mountains and the Ivory Coast are Africa's priority areas for genetic resource preservation through the establishment of protected areas. This will not, however, be possible without greatly accelerated rural development outside the protected areas. What is needed, therefore, is a combined rural development/protected area programme.

Similar measures are required in Asia, where priority should be given to the exceptionally rich lowland (below 300 metres) dipterocarp forests of Borneo, peninsular Malaysia, Sumatra and the Philippines, and in the Americas, where priority should be given to the western Amazon basin, the Pacific coast areas of Colombia and Ecuador, and coastal and south-eastern Brazil. The softwood (coniferous) forests of south-eastern Brazil are projected to decline from 5.8 million hectares (14 million acres) in 1975 to 0.8 million hectares (2 million acres) in 2000 (a loss of 86 per cent).[29] Softwood forest depletion is also serious in central America (20 per cent loss) and the Caribbean (22 per cent).[29] Since the pine species of these regions provide the genetic raw materials for the afforestation programmes of many other tropical countries, urgent conservation measures are required.

Regions where destruction is less widespread or rapid also need action, although their emphasis will be somewhat different. In such regions there is time to establish networks of protected areas designed systematically to safeguard a comprehensive range of the genetic diversity of tropical forests, especially of the tropical rain forests. These regions are the Caribbean, central Africa, developing Oceania, and parts of South America (notably north of the Amazon) and of continental south-east Asia. In these regions there should also be greater scope for experimental research and management to develop productive, sustainable systems for the utilization of tropical forests.

In all regions there is an acute need to protect areas of unusual genetic diversity, promote rural development based on production systems that enable a high proportion of forest cover to be retained, develop systems of commercial exploitation that utilize products other than timber (such as drugs, gums and resins, and natural silk), and ensure that felling and planting programmes are sustainable. The cooperation of developed countries is required to make sure that their demand for tropical forest products does not exceed the capacity of tropical forest countries to supply them non-destructively.

References

1.Pereira, H C (1973) *Land Use and Water Resources in Temperate and Tropical Climates* Cambridge University Press

2.Das, D C (1977) Soil conservation practices and erosion control in India: a case study. In *Soil Conservation and Management in Developing Countries*; FAO report of an expert consultation held in Rome 22-6 November 1976. *FAO Soils Bulletin* **33**

3. US Agency for International Development (1979) *Environmental and Natural Resources Management in Developing Countries: A Report to Congress, Volume I.* USAID, Department of State, Washington DC

4. Holeman, N (1968) The sediment yield of major rivers of the world. *Water Resources Research* **4**:737-47

5. Sterling, C (October 1976) Nepal. *Atlantic Monthly*

6. Chauhan, S K (1978) The Chipko Movement — Indians who hug their trees. *Earthscan*

7. Myers, Norman (1978) Forests for people. *New Scientist* **80**:951-53

8. Wadsworth, Frank (1978) Deforestation: death to the Panama canal. In *Proceedings of the US Strategy Conference on Tropical Deforestation* US Department of State and US Agency for International Development, Washington DC

9. World Bank (1978) *Forestry: Sector Policy Paper.* World Bank, Washington DC

10. FAO (1977) *FAO Trade Yearbook 1976* (Volume 30) FAO, Rome

11. FAO (1978) *The State of Food and Agriculture 1977* FAO, Rome

12. FAO (1971) *Environmental Aspects of Natural Resources Management:Forestry* FAO Rome

13. Sommer, Adrian (1976) Attempt at an assessment of the world's tropical forests. *Unasylva* **28**:5-24

14. Whitmore, T C (1975) *Tropical Rain Forests of the Far East* Clarendon Press

15. Poore, Duncan (1974) Saving tropical rain forests. *IUCN Bulletin* **5**:29-30

16. Slud, P (1960) The birds of Finca la Selva, Costa Rica, a tropical wet forest locality. *Bulletin of American Museum of Natural History* **121**:49-148

17. Richards, P W (1973) A tropical rain forest. *Scientific American* **229**(6):58-68

18. Salati, E, Marques, J and Malion, L C B (1978) Origen e distribuicao das chuvas na Amazonia. *Interciencia* **3**

19. Woodwell, George M (1978) The carbon dioxide question. *Scientific American* **238**:34-43

20. World Climate Conference (1979) *Declaration and Supporting Documents* World Meteorological Organization, Geneva

21. Lewis, Walter H and Elvin-Lewis, Memory P F (1977) *Medical Botany: Plants Affecting Man's Health*. John Wiley. And Morton, Julia F (1977) *Major Medicinal Plants: Botany, Culture and Users* Charles C Thomas

22. Wells, D R (1971) Survival of the Malaysian Bird Fauna. *Malayan Nature Journal* **24**:248-256

23. Cortes Lombana, A (1975) Soil capability and management in Colombian Amazonia and Orinoquia. In *The Use of Ecological Guidelines for Development in the American Humid Tropics*. IUCN, Gland

24. Sommer, Adrian (1976) Attempt at an assessment of the world's tropical forests. *Unasylva* **28**:5-24

25. Whitmore, T C (1975) *Conservation Review of Tropical Rain Forests, General Considerations and Asia* IUCN, Gland

26. Data from IUCN files

27. Myers, Norman (1979) *The Sinking Ark* Pergamon

28. Allen, Robert (April 1975) Woodman spare that tree. *Development Forum*

29. Lanly, J P and Clement, J (1979) *Present and Future Forests and Plantation Areas in the Tropics*. FO:MISC 79/1. FAO, Rome

Chapter 4

Learning to live on planet sea

With uncanny accuracy, wastes from an Italian metal refinery are being dumped in the only part of the Mediterranean where summer after summer fin whales come to feed. The dumping has been linked to ship collisions with dying or incapacitated whales and to discoveries of dead stranded whales, with large sections of skin destroyed or loaded with sulphur and heavy metals.[1]

The whales feed in the area (off Corsica) because it is exceptionally productive. Tiny floating plants multiply explosively in regular blooms, and these blooms support equally dramatic increases in the shrimp-like animals which are the fin whales' food. It is an odd place to dump poisons even if the fin whales did not go there. The Mediterranean is not a particularly fertile sea, and what patches of productivity exist there need careful protection.

As the ocean covers seven-tenths of our planet, it might more aptly have been called 'sea' rather than 'earth'. Yet the sea is apparently so foreign to us that such perverse behaviour as that described above is symptomatic of the way we treat it. Marine management is still extremely unsophisticated, lagging far behind our (admittedly inadequate) knowledge of the seas. Often human activities that have an impact on the sea are scarcely regulated at all. But when they are, management is fragmented and quite inadequate as a means of controlling the multiple ways we use marine resources. One management authority may regulate pollution; another fishing; and yet another the catching of marine mammals like whales or seals.

The life of the seas is not so divided. It has its own special dynamic, a rhythm dramatically illustrated by the feeding behaviour of whales. The whales, like all sea animals, depend on the periodic blooms of plankton, which are largely regulated by temperature changes. In the spring and early summer, Pacific fin whales feed on minute planktonic animals called copepods. When the waters warm to more than 8 degrees centigrade (46 degrees fahrenheit), the copepods 'migrate' downwards to levels the whales cannot reach, and the fins move north to colder pastures.

The life of the Bering Sea is a gigantic gamble in which the chips are a maximum of two plankton blooms a year. Egg-laying by fish is synchronized with the blooms. The eggs drift towards the bloom areas and by the time the larvae hatch and need food, they are over the areas when the blooms occur. Not surprisingly, failure is the norm but enough fish survive to support 450,000 tonnes of marine mammals and 14,500 tonnes of sea and coastal birds.[2]

Unhappily, human beings now threaten to undermine this system by competing directly for the fish. Already, most food fish stocks are fully or over-exploited, and harvests of pollack (the most important fish species) have exceeded maximum sustainable yield every year since 1970.[2]

Food from the wild

The world's most valuable wild animals are almost certainly shrimps. Their closest rivals are cod and herring. The total annual value of exports of fresh and frozen shrimp from developing to developed countries is already close to $1000 million. The US shrimp catch alone is worth more than $200 million a year. The world annual export values of the herring and cod families are each well over $700 million. If the value of domestic consumption is added these animals are also each worth more than $1000 million a year.[3] These animals are the bearers of flesh more valuable than ivory and costlier than furs. But they illustrate an often overlooked fact: the wild creatures of the sea are big business.

There are no world figures for domestic trade in fish and fishery products, but it is clear from export figures alone that trade in seafood is both substantial and rapidly growing. In 1978 seafood exports reached almost $11,000 million, an increase of 15 per cent over the previous year.[4]

Nineteen countries, six of them developing (Mexico, Peru, India, Thailand, Indonesia and South Korea), each earn $100 million or more a year from fish exports. Norway, Canada and Denmark each earn more than $600 million a year from their seafood exports. Seventeen countries, all but three (Iceland, Norway, Denmark) developing, each derive 3 per cent or more of their export earnings from seafood. Peru, Senegal and the Solomon Islands depend on fish for 10 per cent or more of their export trade, and Iceland's dependence on seafood exports is as high as 78 per cent.[5]

The life of the sea provides city dwellers with their last link with humanity's oldest and longest-lasting way of life: that of the hunter-gatherer. The human species has lived by hunting and gathering its food for more than 99 per cent of its time on earth. Today, the cod in the fish fingers and the skate and plaice in the fish and chips of the English, the herring so beloved of the Scandinavians, the sashimi of Japan, the crabs that are the justifiable pride of Maryland and Virginia, and the shrimp in the shrimp cocktails found in every 'international' restaurant in the world are still hunted or gathered. The technologies may be those of the space age but the techniques are those of the stone age.

The fish and other animals of the sea are the last major resource to be exploited in this way. Although the farming of freshwater fish, particularly trout and carp, is well established, the farming of marine animals is still in its infancy. Most mariculture (as sea farming is sometimes called) is not farming at all but assisting wild animals through critical stages in their lives or providing them with a bigger area of favourable environment than exists normally.

On average, fish and other seafood account for 6 per cent of the total protein and 17 per cent of the animal protein in the human diet. If this seems small, it should be remembered that on a world basis most (65 per cent) protein comes from plants, chiefly cereals, beans and peas, nuts and oilseeds. Meat accounts for 16 per cent and milk products for 9.5 per cent of the average total protein intake.[6]

These averages conceal substantial differences between and within countries. Thirty-two countries get 34 per cent or more of their animal protein from seafood, and another 11 countries consume double the world average for seafood consumption. The main seafood consuming countries (calculated on the bases of *per capita* consumption and dietary importance rather than on the basis of gross consumption) are all in the tropics. They are located principally in south-east Asia, the western central Pacific, west Africa, and the Caribbean, with the exceptions of Japan, North and South Korea, Portugal, Spain, Iceland, Denmark and Norway.[6] The main catching countries include many more from the wealthier northern hemisphere, but a number of developing countries are now great fishing nations as well.

International statistics are a little misleading. Many communities in countries not otherwise notable for fish eating depend heavily on seafood, whether for subsistence, income or both. Besides, the cultural and aesthetic importance of seafood is at least as great and possibly much greater than its nutritional importance. What dish is more symbolic of expensive luxury than caviar?

The problems

Overfishing

Unfortunately use of fisheries is often not sustainable and their contribution to national diets and incomes is likely to diminish. The result of past and present overfishing is that the annual world catch is 15 to 20 million tonnes (or about 20 to 24 per cent) *lower* than it might otherwise have been.[7] At least 25 of the world's most valuable fisheries are seriously depleted.[8] Many more are now so fully exploited that they can be expected to become depleted within a decade or so, because of the effects of exploitation either alone or in combination with those of pollution and habitat destruction.

The consequences of such over-exploitation can be illustrated from the north-west Atlantic, where, because of overfishing in the late 1960s, cod catches are still only a third of their estimated potential. The drops in cod, herring and haddock catches (all caused by overfishing) could not be compensated for by increased catches of capelin and mackerel, and the total catch of the fishery as a whole has declined from 4.3 million tonnes in 1970 to 3.5 million tonnes in 1976.[8]

The story of the north-east Atlantic herring has become a classic of wilful over-exploitation. The first time (the 1974-75 season) the

North-East Atlantic Fisheries Commission (NEAFC) fixed a total allowable catch (TAC) for the North Sea stock of herring, it was much higher (at 500,000 tonnes) than that recommended by the International Council for the Exploration of the Seas (ICES), the Commission's scientific advisor. Subsequently, a TAC of 250,000 tonnes was agreed for the period July 1975 to December 1976. However, Denmark and Iceland objected on the grounds that their shares were too small, and so *all* restrictions were lifted throughout the second half of 1975. A TAC of 87,000 was agreed for the first half of 1976, followed by a total ban, but by the second half of 1976 even a TAC of 87,000 was rejected. It was not until a year later a ban was agreed. In a single decade the North Sea herring catch fell from 700,000 tonnes a year to 160,000 tonnes, 'regulated' by quotas too high even to slow the decline and consistently higher than those recommended by ICES.[9]

The lesson of the North Sea herring has not yet been learned. But for the lucky survival of a small number of fry born in 1969, another north-east Atlantic herring fishery, the Atlanto-Scandian, might have been extirpated. Some individuals survived to spawn in 1973, however, and the spawning stock is rebuilding. Nevertheless it is still very low, and ICES has recommended that the ban on fishing be continued. Despite this recommendation, Norway intends to resume fishing (albeit at a low level).[9]

Although there is local overfishing in all regions, over-exploitation is generally most pronounced in regions dominated by developed countries. Five of the eight regions where fish stocks are under heaviest pressure are developed: north-west Atlantic, north-east Atlantic, Mediterranean, north-west Pacific, north-east Pacific. Of the remaining three, two — eastern central Atlantic and south-east Atlantic — are dominated by developed country fishing fleets. France, Japan, Norway, Spain and the USSR are dominant in the eastern central Atlantic (with South Korea operating the only major developing country fleet). Japan, Poland, Spain, the USSR and South Africa operate the largest fleets in the south-east Atlantic (with Cuba operating the sole major developing country fleet). The single exception is the south-east Pacific, where most of the fishing is done by Peru and Chile.[8]

Over-exploitation is waste: the substitution of relatively small short-term gains for much bigger medium to long-term losses. A sobering measure of this wastage is the conversion over the years of poor people's food into rich people's food. There was a time in the UK, before over-exploitation and pollution did their work, when oysters and fresh salmon were a monotonously common feature of the poor person's diet. This is no longer the case and both are now beyond the pocket of the average family. Now the cod, which as fish fingers has become the staple of economical British suppers, seems to be going in their direction. As overfishing makes cod scarce, its price goes up, and the fishing industry now warns that the British public must accept 'unconventional' fish in its fish fingers. It would be a sad day if scarcity were to give cod the cachet of lobster.

Accidental killing

Yet an even bigger waste is the accidental capture and killing of non-target animals. For every tonne of shrimp landed at least three tonnes of fish are thrown away dead. This is probably an underestimate.[10] In the Gulf of Mexico the ratio of fish discards to caught shrimp ranges from 3:1 to 20:1, largely depending on whether the shrimp are trawled inshore or offshore.[10] In 1976 the world catch of shrimp was 1.3 million tonnes.[11] Even assuming that some of the fish caught with them were landed and marketed, it is still likely that at least 6.5 million tonnes of fish were destroyed by shrimp trawling alone. Countries such as India are probably losing 980,000 tonnes of fish a year, Thailand 548,000 tonnes a year, Mexico and Indonesia each 360,000 tonnes a year, and so on. A lot of protein is being needlessly wasted.

Accidental killing of non-target animals, though not an exclusively marine problem, is particularly acute at sea. It has brought one species of sea turtle to the verge of extinction, prevented or slowed the recovery of several fish stocks, and is damaging many populations of dolphins, porpoises, sea cows, seals and seabirds. The problem is known technically as incidental take, and that is all it would be if the animals taken incidentally were not crushed in the nets or drowned and if more than a tiny fraction of them were used instead of being thrown away.

Although the survival of relatively few species — five sea turtles, one porpoise, and all four sea cow species — is threatened by incidental take, the problem has grown so widespread and destructive that it ranks in severity with pollution and other forms of habitat degradation as a threat to living marine resources.[12]

A million seabirds are killed incidentally every year, and more whales are taken by accident than deliberately.[13] Salmon gill-net fisheries in the north Atlantic and north Pacific destroy annually hundreds of thousands of seabirds and more than 20,000 porpoises.[14]

In 1976 the eastern Pacific tuna fishery took almost 144,000 dolphins, though in the last two years the tuna fleet has shown that the incidental take of dolphins can be sharply reduced.[15]

The symbol of the sorry effects of incidental take is without doubt the Atlantic ridley turtle. The Atlantic ridley is the most endangered of the world's sea turtles. The number of nesting females fell from 40,000 in 1954 to 2000 in 1970, dropping further to 1200 in 1974. By 1977, a mere 400 to 500 females came ashore to breed at Rancho Nuevo in the Gulf of Mexico, virtually the only nesting site for this turtle in the world. In a mere 30 years the species had been cut from 40,000 to 400.[16]

Incidental take of fish causes management problems in many parts of the world. The Pacific halibut was seriously depleted by overfishing during the early 1960s. Today, 15 years later, catches by Canada and the USA are still only half those for the mid-1960s despite efforts to conserve stocks. Incidental catches of juvenile halibut by trawlers fishing for other fish have been blamed for the failure of the species to recover. The US and Canadian governments have imposed restrictions on foreign fishermen in the Bering Sea and the Gulf of Alaska, which appear to have significantly reduced the incidental take of halibut. Nevertheless the problem is still serious enough to cause concern among halibut fishermen and the International Pacific Halibut Commission.[17]

The industrial fisheries of the North Sea and other parts of the north-east Atlantic take tens of thousands of 'immatures' of non-target species, not only herrings but also haddock, whiting and other cod-like fishes. These are undersized fishes which cannot be taken legally by fishermen who fish for human food. The result is a waste of money and a waste of food.[9]

As one commentator has pointed out, the industrial fisheries of the north-east Atlantic

> bring in 2.2 million tons of fish for fish meal, an investment of considerable value. Fish meal is needed to feed cattle and pigs and an industrial fishery which harms no protected species often uses a resource which would otherwise not be used at all. But it must be remembered that 300,000 tons of Norway pout for industrial purposes are worth less than the 20,000 tons of haddock caught among them had they been allowed to grow and join the adult fishery for human consumption. The essential problem is to discover how fisheries for protected species and those for fish meal can coexist.[9]

The problem is even more complex than that. Fisheries for shrimp must also coexist with sea turtles and local fisheries for fish.

Similarly, fisheries for food fish must also coexist with seabirds and marine mammals.

Destruction of coastal wetlands

It can no longer be assumed that depleted fish stocks will recover to their full potential. There are three factors obstructing their recovery. First, the spawning fishes and juveniles may continue to be caught by industrial fisheries (which take fish for conversion to animal feed). Second, ecosystem dynamics can change and another species may take over because the depleted species can no longer compete effectively with it. Third, habitats essential for spawning or as nurseries are being degraded or destroyed outright.

Even apparently unproductive areas such as estuaries, mangrove swamps, salt marshes and other coastal wetlands are crucial for food production. With too much water for a picnic and too much land for a swim, wetlands are cherished only by such apparently unnecessary creatures as coots and ornithologists. But two-thirds of the world's fisheries are directly dependent on the incredible store of fertility hidden in these deceptively uniform environments.

Most of the organic matter produced by coastal wetlands is carried out into the waters of the estuary. The ebb tide in salt marsh creeks contains 30 times more organic matter than open sea, and more than half of it is transported to the nursery and feeding areas of important commercial fish.[18]

Coastal wetlands and seagrass meadows also act as nursery areas to some species. The young of many valuable shrimp species breed at sea, then move into wetlands or seagrass meadows where they seek both food and shelter. Cod, herring, plaice and sole spawn in the open areas of the sea, but their young migrate to estuaries where they spend one or two years before moving back to sea to grow still larger and be caught.

According to a joint study by the German, Dutch and Belgian fisheries research institutes, the Wadden Sea, Europe's largest coastal wetland, supports 58 per cent of the North Sea population of brown shrimp, 53 per cent of its sole, 80 per cent of its plaice, and almost 100 per cent of the North Sea population of herring at some stage in their life cycles. The landed value of these fish is some $140 million a year.[19] In the USA, a 1970 study by the Fish and Wildlife Service estimated the final market value of estuary-dependent or associated fish at $11,000 million annually.[20]

Despite their essential role in the maintenance of fisheries, and hence their large and continuous contribution to a great many national economies, coastal wetlands throughout the world are systematically being wrecked. Estuaries, mangroves, salt marshes and lagoons are being removed or polluted, shrinking inexorably before humanity's growing demand for space to grow food, build houses, dock tankers, erect factories and dump garbage.

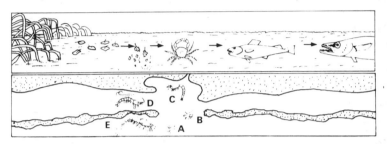

Coastal wetlands and marine fisheries. Coastal wetlands provide nutrients and nurseries for many important fisheries. The top illustration shows the flow of nutrients (highly simplified) from a mangrove swamp to offshore fisheries. The illustration below shows aspects of the life history of several commercially valuable species of shrimp: the eggs (A) are laid offshore, the larvae (B) move inshore, juveniles (C) and adolescents (D) then shelter and feed in mangrove swamps, estuaries and lagoons, before returning to sea as adults (E).

Of the 57 wetlands of acknowledged international importance in the Mediterranean area, only five have any sort of protection.[21] The US Fish and Wildlife Service's 1970 National Estuary Study calculated that 23 per cent of the estuaries of the United States are severely degraded and another 50 per cent are moderately degraded. During the last 20 years, some half a million acres of US coastal wetlands have been lost to dredging and filling operations alone. They continue to be destroyed at a conservatively estimated rate of between 0.5 and 1 per cent of the total area each year.[20]

There are few reliable figures for other countries, but it is unlikely that rates of degradation and destruction throughout the rest of the world are slower. Everywhere prime habitats such as tidal flats, marshes and shallows are being filled in for industry (especially the petrochemical industry), housing, recreation and airports; and estuaries are dredged to create, deepen or improve harbours.

Wetland destruction is rife in both the industrial countries of

79

temperate regions and the developing countries of the tropics. Two examples of extensive misuse of wetlands — one concerning the Wadden Sea, the other the Indian Ocean coasts of Sri Lanka, western India and Pakistan — will demonstrate the scale and intensity of the problem in each group of countries.

Industrial pollution, large-scale 'reclamation' (which simply means draining and filling in), insensitive tourism, and military molestation are the main threats to the Wadden Sea. This immense complex of wetlands is severely polluted, both accidentally and regularly. Large quantities of mercury have escaped from a pharmaceutical plant at Grindsted into Denmark's Ho Bugt area; the River Elbe carries a heavy load of sewage and industrial wastes, especially from Hamburg; and five square kilometres of chemical and electro-metallurgical industries pollute the Ems-Dollard estuary in the Netherlands.[19]

Probably the most dangerous source of pollution of the Dutch part of the Wadden Sea is the River Rhine. The Rhine's waters, together with those of the Meuse and Scheldt, move northwards along the Dutch coast and enter the Wadden Sea through its tidal entrance channels. The Rhine's devastating effect has been demonstrated by extremely large mortalities of sandwich terns and eider ducks in the western Wadden Sea. Heavy metals and other toxic compounds from the industries of the Netherlands, Germany, Switzerland and France continue to enter the Wadden Sea via the Rhine.

Large-scale industrial developments are planned or under construction in Germany and the Netherlands which could endanger the Wadden Sea through reclamation or pollution. For example, in Germany a 700 Mw nuclear power station at Brunsbuttel is starting production this year, and a 1000 Mw nuclear power plant at Brokdorf is in the planning stage. Three new chemical works and a paper mill are also planned or under construction. In the Netherlands some 10 square kilometres (4 square miles) of salt marsh and tidal flats at Emshaven have been reclaimed for the construction of a deep-water harbour and industrial facilities, including a fossil-fuel power station and probably a large petrochemical works. To the south-east of the Ems-Dollard estuary, the establishment of a further 3.5 square kilometres (1.4 square miles) of chemical industries is being considered.

Growing numbers of visitors to the islands of the Wadden Sea disturb birds and seals, erode the dunes and salt marshes, and encourage the development of blocks of holiday homes, yachting marinas, roads and other tourist structures. The western Wadden Sea is also extensively used for military exercises. The western sides of Vlieland and Terschelling Islands, for example, are the targets of tens of thousands of training attacks by NATO aircraft.

The threats to the wetlands of the non-industrial tropics are rarely so sophisticated. According to an IUCN survey of the coasts of Sri Lanka, western India and Pakistan, Sri Lanka's estuaries are just silting up, clogged by the results of erosion inland. 'Bad land-use practices, particularly deforestation, cause this erosion...The rivers run red with silt. Riverborne soil is clogging up Negombe Lagoon — considered the most productive of Sri Lanka's estuaries — and smothering habitats important to fisheries.'[22]

A widespread problem along the coasts of Sri Lanka and India is the cutting of mangroves for firewood, livestock fodder and building materials. The IUCN survey describes two areas where the problem is particularly severe:

> In Sri Lanka's Jaffna district there are five enormous, extremely shallow, interconnecting estuaries. The mangroves along the northern estuary are cut for firewood and removed in oxcarts. The underlying mud and leaves are exposed to direct sun and soon dry hard. In this way, important shrimp and crab habitat is lost and the contribution of leaf-fall to fish and prawn production is reduced.
> Okha, at the southwest end of the Gulf of Kutch, India, is an area remarkably rich in intertidal organisms and is one of India's biological showpieces. Corals, estuarine crocodiles, otters, turtles, dugongs, dolphins and flamingoes are all found in the Gulf, and numerous birds nest in the mangroves of the southern shore. This area contains the best examples of mangrove forest on the western seaboard of India. The mangrove trees are being cut for firewood, and corals are being dredged from the Gulf to feed a nearby cement factory.

However, the plight of Pakistan's Indus delta shows that the problems facing the Wadden Sea are coming to the Indian Ocean. The IUCN survey reports that:

> industrial and agricultural pollution seriously threatens the productivity of certain of the delta's estuaries. Already rivers are polluted by agrochemicals, and the installation by Russians of a steel mill near Phitti creek could upset the adjacent shrimp nursery grounds. A vast acreage of mangrove is to be dredged or filled in during the construction of a new port for Karachi.

Destruction of fisheries could cause enormous hardship. Phitti and Korangi creeks annually produce more than 800 metric tons of prawns. The Indus delta prawn fishery is one of Pakistan's most valuable fisheries, a major source of foreign exchange, giving employment to thousands of local people.

The Indus delta's situation is the Wadden Sea's with a crucial difference. Scientists and resource managers concerned with the fate of the Wadden Sea have the resources to predict the effects of pollution and of the construction of ports and industries, and therefore have the ammunition with which to prevent (or at least minimize) them. Pakistan's resource managers do not have these resources. Diari creek, flowing into Manora bay, Karachi, carries the effluents of more than 100 industries, but the Fisheries Department has neither the money nor the technical facilities to carry out adequate impact studies. The Director of Fisheries for Sind is particularly worried about the possible effects of discharges from the proposed steel mill, but lacks information on which to base cogent scientific arguments against its construction.

Habitat degradation and removal are already significant problems for the fisheries of the USA, causing losses of almost $86 million every year.[23] Off the east coast 87 per cent of the total economic damage is done to two regions: the Gulf of Mexico, from the southern tip of Florida to the Mexican border, and the middle Atlantic area from Long Island, New York, down to and including Chesapeake Bay.

The two main problems in the Gulf of Mexico are dredging and filling of coastal wetlands and closures of shellfish beds for public health reasons because of sewage contamination. Since an estimated 97 per cent of the species in commercial catches in the Gulf of Mexico depends on estuaries, wetland destruction has a disastrous effect. It has been calculated that for every acre (0.4 hectare) of estuary 'reclaimed' or otherwise destroyed, there is a corresponding loss of production on the continental shelf of almost 1000 kilograms (2200 pounds) of fish. Every year 67,000 hectares (165,000 acres) of prime estuary habitat in the Gulf of Mexico are removed. This constitutes 5.5 per cent of the total area of prime habitat and almost 3 per cent of the region's entire coastal wetland area.[24]

Pollution

Wetland destruction is also a major problem along the middle Atlantic coast but it is overshadowed by direct kills of fish and other marine animals. Heavy recurrent pollution of the New York Bight is responsible for an unusually high incidence of fin rot disease in winter flounder and of 'shell disease' in American lobster and rock crab. Massive kills are caused by recurrences of anoxic conditions, ie severely reduced dissolved oxygen levels due to excessive inputs of nutrients, largely via municipal wastewater discharges. Billions of organisms, including lobsters, surf clams, crabs, hake, winter flounder and sea bass, have been killed by these conditions. Other fish kills are due to municipal or industrial discharges. In Virginia in 1973, 7.5 million fish were killed in one incident due to over-chlorination of waste effluent. The total cost of fish, crustacean and mollusc kills in the region is estimated to be $14.5 million a year.[24]

Elsewhere in the world the problems are less well documented but are probably as severe. In the Mediterranean, which with only 1 per cent of the world ocean surface has an estimated 50 per cent of all the floating oil and tar, oil pollution has not only fouled beaches and fishing gear, but has tainted many fish and molluscs (such as grey mullet and mussels in Spain) and begun to have an impact on fish populations. Spiny lobsters have been killed by oil off Tunisia, and the spawning grounds of bonito and mackerel off Turkey have been seriously affected.[25]

The Bay of Muggia in the north of the Adriatic Sea, formerly rich in fish and molluscs, has been devastated by petrochemical wastes. Oil pollution in the Adriatic is claimed to have reduced the numbers of dolphins. The oil, broken down into soluble fractions, is taken up by zooplankton (small floating animals), which are eaten by mackerel. These, in turn, are eaten by the dolphins.[1]

Marine pollution in Japan is rising rapidly. Before 1970 there were fewer than 400 pollution incidents a year, but since 1972 there have been more than 2200 annually. The biggest source of pollution comes from oil tankers and other vessels which deliberately or accidentally discharge oil. But sewage and industrial pollutants are also significant.[26]

Pollution can have two effects on fisheries. It can change yields, increasing or reducing them depending on the type and amount of pollutant, or it can make seafood unfit for sale. Despite the notorious experience of minamata disease, mercury levels in fish and shellfish landed at several Japanese ports are still too high. A 1973 survey revealed that 22 per cent of the species in Minamata Bay, 18 per cent in Tokuyama Bay, 29 per cent on the waterfront at Naoezu, and 26 per cent of the species in Kagoshima Bay had mercury levels exceeding the provisional control limit of 0.4 parts per million (ppm).

In Japan the effect of pollution on fishery yields fluctuates. Recently outbreaks of red tides have increased sharply, apparently as a result of over-enrichment of relatively enclosed areas due to an increase in the discharge of municipal and industrial wastes. In 1973, 27 cases of red tide-related damage, costing $1.97 million, were reported. The cost of 33 cases in 1972, however, was $24.6 million. Forty-one of the 58 cases of damage due to oil pollution reported in 1973 cost $5.89 million, though this was less than the damage to fisheries caused by oil pollution in the two previous years.

Although marine pollution in Japan is responsible for expensive episodes of destruction, it does not appear to have reduced yields yet. Fisheries production in the Seto Inland Sea, for example, has risen steadily since the late 1920s. The composition of the catch has changed, however, and this change has probably been caused by pollution. Catches of red sea bream, shrimp and swimming crab — all important Seto species — have declined drastically since 1953, because of a combination of the effects of industrial and municipal discharges and land 'reclamation'. By contrast, apparently because of increases in nutrients from sewage and agricultural run-off, catches of anchovy, sand lance, flatfish, conger eels, cuttlefish, sea cucumbers and short-necked clams have gone up. So too has production of the larvae of herring-like species. At present, therefore, the beneficial effects of present levels of enrichment appear to outweigh the damage caused by other forms of pollution and the filling in of wetlands.

This situation is unlikely to last if the waters continue to be over-fertilized by human wastes. Once they reach a critical level, ordinary organic wastes like sewage can disrupt fish feeding and nursery grounds in a number of ways. Oxygen can be so reduced that adults are forced out of the area. Eggs are either prevented from hatching or (if they hatch) the larvae are unable to develop. Food organisms may be replaced by organisms that are tolerant of pollution but which the fish do not eat. Larval development can be hindered or stopped altogether if there are growths of injurious bacteria or the water becomes too cloudy.

Destruction of coral reefs

Such problems are not restricted to coastal wetlands. In many parts of the world coral reefs are also under attack from destructive fishing methods (including the use of dynamite), excessive collection of corals, shells and other coral organisms, extraction of coral sand from lagoons, development of lagoons, oil pollution, siltation from erosion inland, pesticides, heat pollution, brine pollution (from desalination plants) and sewage pollution. Entire reefs in the

Philippines have been removed for building foundations and roads. Reefs near towns have been stripped of corals for ornament, and those near sugar refineries have been severely degraded. In Sri Lanka repeated removal of coral reef for the production of lime is so extensive that a local fishery has collapsed; mangroves, small lagoons and coconut groves have disappeared; and local wells have been contaminated with salt.[27]

Coral reefs are the tropical rain forests of the sea. Like the rain forests, coral communities scavenge and hoard the nutrients of an impoverished environment and create a fantastically diverse array of exotic creatures. Among them are animals that are increasingly likely to play a role in the discovery and development of new pharmaceuticals. Hoffmann La Roche in Australia and Hoechst in Brazil are already exploring the chemical novelties to be found in coral reefs. At the same time coral reefs have a more direct contribution to the lives and livelihoods of millions of coastal communities. They provide critical habitats for the fish on which many of them depend, and protect the coast. Indeed, without the activities of corals and other reef-building organisms, more than 400 islands would not exist.[28]

Reef-building corals can survive only in shallow, clear waters, where sufficient sunlight can penetrate for photosynthesis by the algae with which they coexist. These algae, called zooxanthellae, live within the coral animals' tissues and help them secrete the calcium carbonate which covers their bodies and forms the reef. When deprived of zooxanthellae for long periods, corals die.

Water cloudiness is therefore a serious threat to coral reefs and one that is growing. In its most extreme form, cloudiness becomes sedimentation, ie the deposition of silt carried down by rivers and streams. Corals have long had to contend with this and can rid themselves of normal amounts of falling sediment. But reckless forestry, farming and ranching have greatly increased erosion and the loads carried to the sea.

Millions of tonnes of valuable soil are deposited in lagoons in the Virgin Islands, Hawaii, Australia, Tanzania and elsewhere, killing the corals and destroying entire reef communities. Dumping and dredging also cause irreparable damage. Large-scale dredging in French Polynesia, by raising clouds of fine sediment for long periods, has already destroyed important sections of reefs.

Coral reefs, like many other sensitive coastal environments, increasingly suffer from sewage pollution. The best known example is Kaneohe Bay in the Hawaiian island of Oahu. Described 48 years ago as 'one of the most favourable localities' for coral growth, more than 99 per cent of the corals at the sound end of the bay have been killed by the 11,000 cubic metres (more than 14,000 cubic yards) of sewage that enter the bay every day.[29]

More local, but generally even more devastating than sewage, is waste heat pollution. Many coral species die if exposed for up to 24 hours to a temperature of 5 - 6 degrees centigrade (9 - 10 degrees fahrenheit) higher than normal. Prolonged temperature increases of only 3 degrees centigrade (5 degrees fahrenheit) can also kill these corals.[29] Not surprisingly, then, waste heat from power stations has devastated a number of reefs, especially in Florida.

The case of the open ocean

The open ocean — the sea beyond national jurisdiction — is part of the global commons: that part of the planet that belongs to nobody, and hence to everybody. Because nobody own it, however, it is exploited even more carelessly than are coastal waters. Only distance from shore saves the open ocean from the worst kinds of pollution and habitat destruction. But the advent of deep-sea mining will almost certainly change that.

Much of the open ocean remains frontier country in which people can exploit living resources as they please as long as they have the technology to do so. While the open ocean is not as biologically rich as continental shelf areas it includes unique ecosystems and provides some (and in some cases all) of the critical habitats of several culturally and economically important groups of animals, notably whales and tunas. Species that are confined to the open ocean are the common resource of all humanity; species that move between the open ocean and waters under national jurisdiction are shared resources. Special provision for the conservation of both groups of species is therefore needed, but it does not really exist.

Whaling, for example, is regulated by the International Whaling Commission (IWC), but the IWC's efforts have been so feeble that it has been unable to prevent the decline of the great whales, or of the commercial whaling industry which is now almost at an end. Attempts at whale conservation almost invariably have been a case of too little too late. Blue, bowhead, grey, humpback and right whales were exploited to critically low levels before being given protection, and still the north-west Pacific stock of humpback whales and the north-west Atlantic stocks of blue whales and right whales may not survive. Since 1969 annual quotas for fin, sei, and Bryde's whales in the North Pacific have been consistently higher than catches. Indeed, in most years, the catches were less than the quotas for the following year.[30] So the IWC's quota system has failed to regulate catches, and has not prevented the steady decline of the whales.

Although management by the IWC has improved recently, it is still grossly inadequate. Rates of increase of some species are probably lower than is assumed, and insufficient account is taken of our woeful ignorance of (amongst other things) whale behaviour. For example, we do not know what effect killing the older, larger animals has on whale societies. But the most serious deficiency is that no attempt is made to relate the harvesting of whales with that of other marine mammals and of the fish on which they feed, or to link the effects of catches with those of other human impacts on the sea such as pollution. The result is that in any given region the assumed potential catch of any species is likely to be put too high.

As the numbers of whales have dwindled to ever more perilous levels, so whale lovers and concerned scientists have clamoured increasingly for an end to whaling altogether, or at least for a moratorium on all commercial whaling. In 1979, the IWC went some way towards meeting this need by imposing a partial moratorium on whaling by factory ships or whale catchers attached to factory ships. Only one whale species, the minke whale, can now be taken in this way. The IWC has also designated as a sanctuary almost the entire area of the Indian Ocean. In this sanctuary area *all* commercial whaling is prohibited until 1989. This is an encouraging step forward, but it needs to be matched by international measures to protect the whales' habitats.

The Southern Ocean

The Southern Ocean is the body of water surrounding Antarctica. Its outer boundary is the Antarctic Convergence (the well defined but fluctuating line where the cold surface waters of the polar seas sink beneath the warmer waters of the Atlantic, Indian and Pacific Oceans). The Southern Ocean is the least exploited of all the oceans, but the carve-up is beginning. Soviet and Japanese fleets have already begun fishing for krill, tiny shrimp-like animals that swarm in the cold waters in enormous quantities. It is said that the krill catch could rise from about 50,000 tonnes in 1977-78 to 60 million tonnes or more a year, thereby doubling the world's total annual catch of all aquatic animals. Not surprisingly, therefore, krill have been described as the world's largest source of untapped protein.[31] But this food source is not entirely untapped. Krill are the major food of five species of large

87

whales, including the endangered blue whale and humpback whale, and are also important for three species of seals, many seabird species and several species of fish. The whales, cut down by overhunting, could be despatched into oblivion once and for all if the industrial nations of the world snatch the krill from their mouths. Unless krill exloitation is extremely carefully and conservatively regulated, its effects on other Southern Ocean species could be devastating.

The Southern Ocean confronts us with the choice of developing a civilized system of managing the seas, or of succumbing to a mad scramble to be first in a grand finale of oceanic pillage and rape. The Antarctic Treaty powers are negotiating a convention to regulate the taking of the living resources of the Southern Ocean, but they are doing so behind closed doors and there is no guarantee that they will be responsive to the larger interests of all mankind in this common heritage.

What should be done

A major difficulty in the conservation of marine environments is that they are not self-contained entities but parts of a continuum extending from the land to the open ocean, and from one part of the ocean to another. The oceans have their boundaries, but they are subtle and do not always correspond with popular conceptions of them. Currents, upwellings, salinity and temperature differences can act as barriers. The coast, by contrast, often unites rather than separates land and sea.

Governments and their resource management institutions generally have failed to recognize this phenomenon. Indeed most of the problems facing the life of the seas stem from the failure of human politics and administrations to adjust to the ecological realities of the seas. Thus the decline of fish such as herring is due less to ignorance of the animals' biology or of the environments of which they are part than to the weaknesses of the human institutions governing their exploitation. In many cases the scientific advice on the management of such fisheries has been sound, if a little mealy mouthed. But fishermen vote and governments have often been reluctant, until too late, to take steps that would put some fishermen out of work but would enable the remainder to earn their living from the sea virtually indefinitely.

Like the land the sea is an area of multiple use. It is used to produce food, for transport, mining and quarrying, oil production, recreation and waste disposal. Unlike the land, however, very little attempt is made to manage for multiple use. Such regulatory bodies as exist are generally concerned with a single resource, such as fish. As a result, the seas and their living resources are increasingly being over-exploited and degraded. New organizations are needed, or existing organizations should be modified and given new mandates, to manage marine living resources comprehensively, and in ways that take full account of the vital links between land and sea and between the marine areas of one nation and those of others.

Changes in the international law of the seas make the need for these new or improved organizations still more urgent, and also provide new opportunities for better management of marine living resources. Most nations have extended their national jurisdictions by declaring Exclusive Economic Zones (EEZs) for 200 nautical miles from their shores. Most, if not all, of the remainder are likely to do the same. These moves have radically changed the pattern of world trade in marine products and the context in which marine fisheries are managed. Foreign fleets have been limited by new catch quotas or have been forced to move elsewhere. The flag countries of many fleets have lost export trade, and some have been obliged to import fish to compensate for lower catches. Nations with rich offshore resources have begun to enjoy a corresponding increase in their exports or in their bargaining power.

The establishment of EEZs adds to the incentives for coastal states to protect the habitats critical for fisheries since they now control the fisheries which the habitats support. By protecting the habitats and by ensuring that the fisheries themselves are exploited on a sustainable basis, they will assure both a regular high quality protein supply and often a substantial income. Even if the national fishing fleet is insignificant the state can still benefit considerably by allowing other nations to fish its waters in return for concessions. For example, Morocco has been able to use the bigger bargaining power conferred by its EEZ to persuade foreign companies to supply Moroccan processing plants with sardines caught in its relatively unexploited southern waters. The plants can now operate closer to their total capacity, and the nation can benefit from the larger share of the added value. Fishing rights can also be granted in exchange for access to overseas markets, not only for fishery products but also for other commodities or for manufactured goods.

Saving the whale

The plight of the whales is so acute and management is so inadequate that there should be a moratorium on commercial whaling until the conditions outlined below have been fulfilled.

1. The consequences for the ecosystems concerned of removing large portions of the whales' populations, and such populations' capacity for recovery, can be predicted.
2. Permitted levels of exploitation are safe and an effective mechanism exists for detecting and correcting mistakes in the management of any stock.
3. Member nations of IWC are no longer purchasing whale products from, or transferring whaling technology and equipment to, non-member nations or pirate whaling ships.

It is essential that any regime for the exploitation of the Southern Ocean's living resources should so regulate the krill fishery as to prevent:

1. Irreversible changes in the populations of krill.
2. Permitted levels of exploitation are safe and an effective mechanism exists for detecting and correcting mistakes in the management of any stock.
3. Over-capitalization of krill fishing fleets, which could have severe impacts on fisheries outside the Southern Ocean, due to the need to redeploy the krill fleets during the long Antarctic winter.

The Antarctic Treaty powers and nations fishing or intending to fish the Southern Ocean should exercise extreme restraint on catch levels until understanding of this uniquely productive ecosystem improves. All harvesting should be on an experimental basis as part of a scientific research programme to improve knowledge of krill and of the Southern Ocean as a whole. Current research efforts should be strongly supported, and the collection, analysis and dissemination of biological information should be mandatory. An 'international decade' of Southern Ocean research, focusing particularly on ecological processes, should be initiated as a matter of urgency. Baseline areas where no krill or other living or non-living resources may be taken should be set aside and given complete protection, so that outside impacts can be monitored and evaluated correctly. The dimension and location of these areas should be established according to the best available knowledge of the ecosystems concerned.

Continued investigation into the possible environmental effects of tourism, scientific research, mining and oil exploitation, etc is also required. Meanwhile, since oil degrades extremely slowly in conditions such as those of Antarctica and the Arctic and since operating hazards are very high, the feasibility of oil exploration and exploitation in particular should be approached with the utmost caution.

References

1. FAO/UNEP (1978) *Mammals in the Seas Volume 1* Report of the FAO Advisory Committee on Marine Resources Research working party on marine mammals. *FAO Fisheries Series* **5**(1). FAO Rome

2. ibid

3. FAO (1977) *Yearbook of Fishery Statistics, 1976: Fishery Commodities* (Volume 43). FAO, Rome

4. FAO (1979) Fishery commodity situation and outlook 1978-79. Committee on Fisheries. Thirteenth Session, Rome, 8-12 October 1979, COFI/79/Inf 5

5. FAO (1977) *FAO Trade Yearbook, 1976* (Volume 30). FAO, Rome

6. FAO (1977) Provisional food balance sheets, 1972-74 average. FAO, Rome

7. FAO (1979) Review of the state of world fishery resources. Committee on Fisheries. Thirteenth session, Rome, 8-12 October 1979. COFI/79/Inf 4

8. FAO (1976) Review of the state of exploitation of the world fish resources. Committee on Fisheries. Eleventh Session, Rome, 19-26 April 1977, COFI/77/5. And FAO (1978) Review of the state of world fishery resources. Committee on Fisheries. Twelfth Session, Rome, 12-16 June 1978, COFI/78/Inf 4

9. Cushing, D H (1977) The Atlantic fisheries commissions. *Marine Policy* **1**:230-238

10. Klima, Edward F (1976) A review of the fishery resources in the western central Atlantic. *WECAF Studies* **3** FAO/UNDP

11. FAO (1977) *Yearbook of Fishery Statistics, 1976*: *Catches and Landings* (Volume 42) FAO, Rome

12. IUCN (1975) *Red Data Book* IUCN, Gland

13. Estimate based on a preliminary review by the author of the incidental take problem

14. ICBP (1975) Mortality of sea birds from Japanese salmon gill-nets in the North Pacific. ICBP (US National Section)

15.Anon (1978) Tuna-dolphin facts and figures. *IUCN Bulletin* **9**:6

16.IUCN (1975) *Red Data Book*, **3**:Amphibia and Reptilia. IUCN, Gland. And Anon (1977) Atlantic ridley in deep trouble *IUCN Bulletin* **8**:31

17.FAO (1978) Activities of regional fishery bodies during the intersessional period. Committee on Fisheries. Twelfth session, Rome, 12-16 June 1978, COFI/78/Inf 6

18.Barnes R S K (1974) Estuarine Biology *Institute of Biology's Studies in Biology* **49**

19.Paragraphs on the Wadden Sea are drawn from *IUCN Bulletin* **7**:7-12

20.US Fish and Wildlife Service (1970) *National Estuary Study* US Fish and Wildlife Service, Washington DC

21.Data from IUCN files

22.Salm, R V (1975) Critical marine habitats in Pakistan, western India and Sri Lanka. Unpublished report, IUCN

23.Kumpf, Herman E (1977) Economic impact of the effects of pollution on the coastal fisheries of the Atlantic and Gulf of Mexico regions of the United States of America. *FAO Fisheries Technical Paper*, **172**. And Hester, Frank J (1976) Economic aspects of the effects of pollution on the marine and anadromous fisheries of the western United States of America. *FAO Fisheries Technical Paper* **162**

24.ibid

25.Osterberg, C and Keckes, S (1977) The State of Pollution of the Mediterranean Sea. *Ambio* **6**:321-6

26.Tokyo University Fisheries (1976) An assessment of the effects of pollution on fisheries and agriculture in Japan. *FAO Fisheries Technical Paper* **163**

27.Library of Congress, Science and Technology Division (1978) Draft environmental report on Sri Lanka. Library of Congress, Washington DC

28.Salvat, Bernard (1979) Trouble in paradise, part 2:coral reef parks and reserves. *Parks* **4**:1-4

29.Johannes, R E (1972) Coral reefs and pollution. In Mario Ruiva (ed) *Marine Pollution and Sea Life* Fishing News (Books)

30.Holt, S J (1975) The concept of maximum sustainable yield (MSY) and its application to whaling. FAO Advisory Committee on Marine Resources Research ACMRR/MM/IV/4

31.Everson, Inigo (1977) *The Living Resources of the Southern Ocean* FAO, Rome

Chapter 5

Coming to terms
with our fellow species

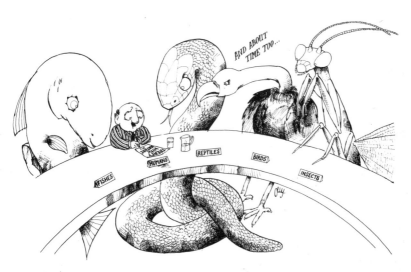

Contemporary people in their species-rich world are like the tenants of a shop full of antique glass who enter it at dead of night during a power cut, slightly drunk. They know roughly where the display tables are, but not well enough to prevent themselves from blundering into them and certainly not to identify the crashes of broken crystal, whether a vase or a bowl, a goblet or a tankard, whether Venetian, Bohemian, or ancient Roman. They scarcely perceive that each crash signifies the loss of something priceless, irreplaceable and uninsured; and they are apparently incapable of taking the elementary precaution of using a flashlight and moving with care.

We do not know how many species we are plunging to extinction. Apart from the higher plants of a few countries, only the larger animals are being monitored sufficiently closely — and then by no means everywhere — for reasonably precise figures to be given. We do know that most of the species have not been evaluated, many have not been described, and some have not even been named. We know, too, that we will never know the full extent of the destruction we are causing. Unique communities with strictly limited regenerative capacities are rapidly contracting before the colonial fires of a desperate peasantry, the explosive explorations of oilmen and mining companies, the behemoths of industrialized forestry, and the persistent nibblings of innumerable goats.

IUCN's *Red Data Book*,[1] the only authoritative source of information on the world's threatened animals, covers only vertebrates (animals with backbones): fish, amphibians, reptiles, birds and mammals. The book lists more than a thousand species and subspecies known to be threatened with extinction: 193 types of fish, 138 amphibians and reptiles, 400 birds and 305 mammals. There are almost certainly more under threat. The *Red Data Book* volume on fish, for example, is weak on tropical America, Africa and Asia where the status of freshwater species is little known. Similarly, we have no means of knowing the status of small and inconspicuous vertebrates in areas such as tropical rain forests that are known to be exceptionally rich in species and are shrinking rapidly.

As for plants, IUCN's Threatened Plants Committee estimated that as many as 25,000 are threatened.[2] This is a guess. But it is an informed guess, based on figures for those parts of the world that have been thoroughly surveyed. There are estimated to be between 200,000 and 250,000 flowering plant species. The imprecision is due partly to the realization that there are species still to be discovered in botanically unexplored regions of the tropics, and partly to differences of opinion among taxonomists (the classifiers of plants) as to which forms in highly variable groups are species and which subspecies or races.

Surveys of the United States by the Smithsonian Institution[3] and of Europe by IUCN's Threatened Plants Committee for the Council of Europe[4] have shown that an average of 10 per cent of the higher plants in those areas are threatened. The proportion is much higher in vulnerable, species-rich habitats such as islands, rain forests, deserts, Mediterranean-type areas, wetlands and coastal sites. For example, almost 18 per cent of the native flora of the Indian Ocean island of Socotra are threatened; and as many as half of Hawaii's higher plants are at risk.

The estimate of 25,000 threatened plant species in the world as a whole is therefore conservative. It does not take account of the grim fact that between 70 and 90 per cent of the world's plant species are in the tropics. These environments, which contain disproportionately more threatened species, are much less able to withstand human pressures than those of the temperate zones. We know that in many parts of the tropics entire communites of rare and unique plants are in danger, but we do not know what those species are, let alone which of them are most imperilled.

We know even less about the lower plants (such as mosses, liverworts, fungi, lichens and seaweeds) or invertebrate animals. There is no question, however, that many of them are in the same plight as the flowering plants and the vertebrates. Habitat destruction is proceeding at such a pace and so many creatures are confined to one or a few areas that species destruction is an almost inevitable by-product. Estimates that attempt to take this factor into account suggest that from half a million to a million species will have been made extinct by the end of this century.

Modern wars are now so destructive, leaving behind them so many unidentified dead, that afterwards it is customary for each of the combatant nations to erect a tomb to the unknown soldier. So rapid is the rate of species loss from habitat removal that it would not be fanciful — indeed it would be sadly appropriate — for those responsible for particularly destructive projects in species-rich areas to erect a tomb to the unknown species.

The problems

Threats to plants

Plants are threatened in one of two main ways: by their wholesale removal by collectors, or by the destruction or alteration of their habitats. Precisely because they are so discriminating, collectors put especially severe pressure on specific groups of plants such as orchids and cactuses. In some cases, the pressure is so great that many species will have disappeared from the wild before we know their relationship with other creatures, notably their pollinators and seed dispersers. Since their pollination and dispersal mechanisms are sometimes bizarre and often highly specialized, not only will a fascinating detail be lost for ever, but an insect or other animal dependent on that plant may also be exterminated.

Collection for trade, however, affects a relatively small proportion of endangered plants. Generally, the greater menace is habitat destruction, the mounting onslaught of bullocks and bulldozers, of machines and domestic animals. The tumultuous proliferation of human numbers and material wants is leading to massive transformations of the world's most sensitive environments: natural forests and grasslands, islands, temperate bogs and marshes, fresh-waters, coasts, estuaries and deserts. At one extreme, the habitats of plants simply disappear, whenever an area of forest is cleared, or a bog is drained, or grassland covered in concrete. At the other, quite subtle alterations can be as disastrous — the enrichment with sewage and fertilizer run-off of freshwaters, or the patter of millions of not-so-tiny feet on beaches, sand-dunes and cliff-tops.

Threats to animals

Habitat destruction is also the main problem for animals. Analysis of the *Red Data Book* shows that 67 per cent of the species listed are threatened by loss or contamination of their habitats. Other important threats are over-exploitation (affecting 37 per cent of species), the effects of introduced exotic species (affecting 19 per cent), competition with people for food (affecting 7 per cent) and accidental killing (affecting 2 per cent of threatened species but having a much wider impact on species that are not yet threatened).[5]

People destroy the habitats of wild animals in astonishingly diverse ways. New or expanded towns, housing, industries, harbours, mines, quarries, cropland, grazing land, and plantations can obliterate vital habitats. Dams can block the spawning migrations of fishes and leave them with too little water downstream and too much upstream (fish can be 'drowned' if they depend on very shallow water for breeding or feeding or if they have adapted to water of a particular heat or chemical composition). Drainage of wetlands and channelization and flood-control measures can deprive aquatic animals of shelter and food. A host of domestic, agricultural and industrial activities can degrade habitats by pollution — or remove them altogether in the course of extracting timber, firewood, building materials. Over-grazing by domestic animals damages the habitats both of land animals and of aquatic ones through, for example, siltation. The catalogue is virtually endless, but the effects are the same: the depletion of species after species and their eventual disappearance altogether.

After habitat destruction, the next greatest causes of extinctions are over-exploitation (see the case study which follows) and the effects of introduced exotic species. Animals and plants introduced into areas where they have not evolved can have a disastrous impact on native creatures. They may compete with the native species for food or simply for space. They may prey on them: the literature of extinct and vanishing species is full of accounts of how introduced mammals, such as rats and cats, or introduced fish, such as bass or rainbow trout, make short work of local animals that have evolved no defences against them. They may destroy habitats directly, as goats and rabbits have done the world over and especially on islands; and they may expose native populations to new diseases, against which they have no resistance, as some introduced birds have done. The species of islands and of freshwaters are particularly vulnerable to the harmful effects of introduced species. It is therefore shocking and a little saddening that government departments that should know better persist in proposing schemes to introduce carp, tilapia and other exotic fishes to help free waterways of weeds or trout and similar species to keep sport fishermen amused.

Over-exploitation means killing more of a species than the species can withstand. Most of the vertebrate species threatened by over-exploitation are found only in developing countries. Only 10 per cent of them occur in the developed world, where the main problems are overfishing and overcollecting for science or pleasure, and the souvenir and pet trades. Prominent victims are five species of sturgeon (two in the USSR, and three in Canada and the USA), the North American cavefishes, the lungless salamanders of the USA, and some of Australia's parakeets.

It is not surprising that the ill-effects of over-exploitation are most pronounced in developing countries. People there still depend on wildlife for food or for the little cash they can get from trade. In many parts of the world, especially in the tropics, wild land mammals, birds and reptiles are the principal sources of meat. In parts of Ghana, Zaire and other countries in west and central Africa, three-quarters of the animal protein comes from wild animals. Among the settlers along Brazil's trans-Amazon highway, wild animals account for up to 20 per cent of the total protein requirements.

Cynics might argue that game is eaten in developing countries because it is cheaper and more readily available than beef, lamb, pork or poultry. This may be so in some cases. But often wild meat is preferred and is eagerly sought. One survey of restaurants in Manaus (Brazil) revealed this list of the top 10 most popular meats (all wild): freshwater turtles, paca, deer, tapir, peccary, armadillo, capybara, wild duck, agouti, tortoise.

Monkeys and rodents are very popular in west Africa. Wildlife biologist Antoon de Vos noted that in 1976 a small monkey carcass cost as much as $7 at the Kisangani market in Zaire. The use of monkeys is so intense that many populations and some species are now threatened by it. Mr de Vos also observes that rodents (especially the giant rat and the cane-rat or grasscutter) are, for several reasons, an unusually valuable source of food. First, they rarely come under game laws and therefore can be taken all the time. Second, they reproduce so rapidly that they can sustain very high yields. Third, they are numerous even in relatively densely populated areas where larger animals are scarce.[6]

Wild plants can also be important sources of food. Two of the most protein-rich plants in the world — the mongongo nut and the tsi bean — are eaten by the San people of Botswana and Namibia. Both these remarkable plants flourish in semi-deserts, and the mongongo nut is particularly prolific. The San practise no agriculture, living traditionally by hunting animals and gathering plants. So abundant and nutritious is the mongongo that one San, when asked why he had not taken to farming, replied: 'Why should we plant, when there are so many mongongo nuts in the world.'[7]

Unfortunately, wild animals in particular are being depleted at an alarming rate, and poaching for food is even more rife than poaching for skins, ivory and other luxuries destined for the industrial world. Wildlife officer Victor Balinga reports on one aspect of the problem he and his colleagues must deal with in Cameroon:

> There are certain main roads which go through national parks, such as the Kalamaloue National Park. Lorry drivers on long-distance routes between Nigeria and Chad will time their journeys in order to arrive at these conservation areas at night, spend some time in illegal hunting and, before morning, be off with their vehicles loaded with meat.[8]

This example is typical of a great many countries.

The case of the international wildlife business

World trade in wildlife and its products is by no means just a matter of local curio shops selling a few souvenirs to tourists. Well-organized commercial enterprises supply a vast and expanding market (mainly industrialized countries) with increasingly scarce 'commodities' taken from the wild (mainly in developing countries). Wildlife is traded dead:

— hides and skins for the luxury fur and leather industry; exotic meat and fish for luxury food; a wide range of other animal and plant products for pharmaceuticals, perfumes, aphrodisiacs, decoration, or investment; specimens for natural history museums;

or alive:

— live animals for the pet trade, zoos and menageries, aquaria and other collections; for the testing of new chemical products, and for biomedical research; live plants for horticulture.

There is big money in the wildlife business, but the people who make it are not the peasants, hunters and poachers but the middlemen or the ultimate sellers who are mostly in Europe or Japan or entrepreneurial centres like Hong Kong and Singapore. In 1979 the estimated turnover for smuggled Australian wildlife was $30 million. Agents with the US Fish and Wildlife Service estimate that the illegal traffic in birds is at least as great as the 350,000 that are legally imported every year. Amazon and African grey parrots, which sold for $300 to $400 each in 1974, fetched $800 each in 1979.[9] Most of the wildlife trade is openly advertised, but a significant part of it takes place on the black markets, often through channels and by methods not unlike those of the drug traffic. The impact of this trade on many species and ecosystems is now serious.

Sea turtles are killed for their leather, tortoise-shell and for soup, as well as to satisfy the apparently insatiable quest for aphrodisiacs. In Mexico, for example, pregnant turtles are killed because the eggs at that stage are considered great aids to sexual potency. Another grotesque trade is that in baby turtles, which are preserved, lacquered and sold as souvenirs to tourists, especially in Mexico, the Caribbean and the Far East.

Six out of the seven sea turtle species are threatened with extinction. Except for the Australian population of the green turtle (*Chelonia mydas*), international trade in all six is now prohibited under CITES, so turtle soup, tortoise-shell and turtle leather is (or shortly will be) banned in all countries party to that treaty (so far 54). However, it will be some time before CITES will bring real relief to sea turtles, since Japan, the leading importer of tortoise-shell, has not yet ratified it. Japan goes as far afield as Fiji, the Solomon Islands, Zanzibar, Aden, Cuba and Nicaragua to get its supplies, consuming between 20,000 and 30,000 hawksbill turtles (*Eretmochelys imbricata*, the source of tortoise-shell) a year.[10]

Trade is making heavy inroads into the populations of many other animals. Small boatloads of walrus heads have been observed in Alaska, the animals decapitated for their valuable tusks. Even the not uncommon practice of making some 'walrus' ivory carvings out of the ivory of African elephants has not prevented the rise in walrus killing. Any animal unfortunate enough to possess large teeth is vulnerable to attack from the trinket trade.

Every year, the Philippines exports from 2 million to 3.5 million tropical marine fish for aquaria. In 1974 Singapore imported (mostly for re-export) more than 39 million aquarium fish. In the same year Tanzania exported 266,700 kg of corals and shells. The Government of Mauritius has expressed concern about the status of the imperial harp shell and of two species of cowrie, one found only in Mauritius and the other confined to Mauritius and Reunion. All three are rare and beautiful, bringing high prices from shell dealers and thus eagerly sought after by local collectors.

Despite Panama's attempts to protect them, hundreds of Panamanian golden frogs are exported to collectors each year. Even greater quantities of baby spectacled caimans (a small American crocodile) are sold either as pets, or stuffed as curios. Thousands of tortoises and turtles are despatched to Europe's pet shops from north Africa and South America. Most of them die within a year because their owners do not know how to look after them.

The pet trade is possibly at its cruellest when exterminating lion-tailed macaque or pileated gibbon mothers so that the juveniles can be captured for sale. Monkeys and apes are also in great demand for entertainment, and their close relationship to man makes them invaluable for biomedical research. Together, zoos, menageries, the pet trade and biomedical research consume an estimated 160,000 to 200,000 primates annually.

The lucrative fur and skin industries impose heavily on otters, the spotted cats, snakes and crocodiles. Many of these animals are increasingly being protected, but the absence of controls in one country often destroys the effectiveness of the controls in others.

Although many Latin American countries forbid hunting and trading in jaguars and ocelots, a substantial trade continues. Some countries leave an easily exploited loophole by permitting the transit or processing of skins imported from elsewhere. Paraguay, Panama, Honduras and Guyana still allow hunting and export of ocelot and jaguar pelts, and with the crude pelts of ocelot fetching up to $100 each and of jaguars $300 each this is a powerful inducement to smugglers from nearby countries.

As particular species decline and as trade in them becomes more restricted so pressure is put on related, more numerous species so that they too become depleted. The scarcity of the exotic cats, for example, has resulted in a boom in the trading of formerly less valued skins like those of bobcats. The growing market for bobcat pelts, now fetching $400 a piece, has encouraged overkill to the point where populations of these small cats are declining noticeably.[11]

Why does wildlife matter?

The history of human use of plant and animal species shows the value of rescuing species from extinction and demonstrates that vanishing and apparently insignificant species can suddenly and unexpectedly become useful and important. The 'pescado blanco' *Chirostoma estor*, a fish which in the wild occurs in a single Mexican lake, was until recently in danger of extinction as a result of overfishing, habitat degradation, and predation and competition by introduced species. Now, as a result of good management and artificial propagation, the fish is being stocked in several reservoirs and dams and a 15 hectare (37 acre) farm is under construction.[12]

When the white settlers of North America cut down the bison from an estimated 60 million to fewer than 600, they destroyed not only one of the greatest wildlife spectacles in the world but also an unparalleled opportunity for commercial meat production.

Well into the nineteenth century when the bison's final slaughter was under way they were so abundant that, at certain seasons, they turned the prairies a uniform black. Even then, naturalists such as John James Audubon were predicting the bison's doom. The Indians were prodigal of the resource, killing frequently for the animals' tongues alone. But the main and most disastrous onslaught was delivered by the white man. Trappers, settlers, train travellers and professional meat hunters slaughtered incredible quantities, Buffalo Bill Cody killing over 4000 in a single year. By 1879, the last survivor of the great southern herd was shot at Buffalo Springs, Texas, on the cattle trail to Santa Fe. Four years later most of the northern herd was rounded up and cut down. So rapid and thorough was the destruction that a rancher who travelled a thousand miles across northern Montana at the time told Theodore Roosevelt that he was 'never out of sight of a dead buffalo, and never in sight of a live one'.

It took no more than half a century to reduce to extinction in the wild a species that even in its last decade numbered millions. Fortunately, some 300 to 600 animals survived to be protected in national parks and wildlife reserves in Canada and the USA. Even today the descendants of what has been described as 'almost certainly the greatest animal congregation that ever existed on earth' are as few as 50,000 to 60,000 in the USA and fewer than 20,000 in Canada.

Yet these animals could become big business. Surplus park-bred bison are now being snapped up by farmers at $700 a head. The reason? They yield better from poorer land and for less trouble than do beef cattle. Bison weigh about 50 per cent more than cattle at maturity, and because they also 'dress' better, more of their carcass can be used commercially (65 per cent compared with 55 per cent). They are easier to care for too, coping well with the harsh prairie winters and foraging for grass and stubble on their own, unlike cattle which have to be tended and fed regularly. Furthermore, bison meat tastes much like beef but is 25 per cent higher in protein and 20 per cent lower in cholesterol. Bison meat is also hypoallergenic (ie it does not cause allergies) and may even provide a clue in the search for a cure to cancer, since bison (unlike cattle) seem not to contract it.[13]

Had some of this information been known to the cattlemen, meat hunters, and trigger-happy train riders (who took pot shots at bison to relieve the monotony of travel) of a hundred years ago, perhaps they might have been less ready to render such a valuable animal almost extinct. The fabled productivity of the prairies might have been even greater today if there were a balanced mixture of cattle ranches and buffalo ranches, the latter costing less to run and able to supply a market undreamed of in the nineteenth century: diet-conscious meat lovers prone to cardiovascular disease.

Wildlife and medicine

Wild plants and animals are essential for modern medicine. They are used directly in the production of medicines and other drugs and as starting materials for drug synthesis, and they contribute indirectly both by providing ideas for chemical compounds that can be synthesized and by helping in the general advance of biological, and hence medical, understanding. According to one analysis, more than 40 per cent of the prescriptions each year in the USA contain a drug of natural origin — either from higher plants (25 per cent) or microbes (13 per cent) or from animals (3 per cent) — as sole active ingredient or as one of the main ones.[14] The same study reports that in the USA alone the value of medicines just from higher plants is about $3000 million a year. Furthermore, of 76 major pharmaceutical compounds obtained from plants, only seven can be synthesized at competitive prices. Reserpine, for example, can be commercially prepared from natural sources for about $0.75 per gram ($21 per ounce), but when synthesized it costs $1.25 per gram ($36 per ounce).[14]

Several developing countries are currently setting up their own pharmaceutical industries in order to supply their peoples with essential drugs at an acceptable cost. As a service to this effort a UN workshop recently compiled a basic list of medicinal plants found in Africa, Asia and Latin America whose active principles are used in modern medicine. More than 40 of the 90 species listed are available only from the wild, and another 20, though cultivated, are also taken from the wild.[15] Preservation of these species and their habitats is thus one of the preconditions for maintaining national pharmaceutical industries.

Important drugs derived from wild plants include colchicine (from *Gloriosa superba*) an anti-inflammatory, anti-gout drug; quinine (from *Cinchona*) used to prevent and treat malaria; the anti-cancer drugs vincristine and vinblastine and the anti-hypertensive drug raubasine (from *Catharanthus*); 1-Dopa (from *Mucuna pruriens*) used against Parkinson's disease; reserpine (from *Rauvolfia*) and vincamine (from *Vinca minor*) both used in the treatment of cardiovascular disease; xanthotoxin (from *Ammi majus*) and Asiaticoside (from *Centella asiatica*) used against skin infections; antispasmodics from *Duboisia myoporoides* and *Hyoscyamus*; cathartics from *Cassia*; ulcer treatments from *Glycyrrhiza glabra*; anti-diarrhoeals from *Berberis aristata*; diosgenin hormones from *Dioscorea* and *Costus speciosus*; solasodine hormones from *Solanum*; muscle-relaxants from *Physostigma venenosum*; eye preparations such as pilocarpine from *Pilocarpus*; and ephedrine (from *Ephedra*) used in the treatment of respiratory diseases.

Medical products from many animal species are also important. Snake venoms are used in non-addictive pain killers, bee venoms in the treatment of arthritis, alantoin from blowfly larvae helps to heal deep wounds, and cantharidin (derived from the European blister beetle) is used to treat certain uro-genital conditions. Ara-A, a compound from a Caribbean sponge (*Tethya crypta*), is effective against herpes encephalitis and has provided a breakthrough in the treatment of diseases caused by viruses, much as penicillin did in the treatment of diseases caused by bacteria.[16] Another compound (ara-C) from this animal is a powerful inhibitor of several cancers, including leukaemia.[17] Squalene from shark liver oil is used as a bactericide to kill harmful bacteria and also in the manufacture of skin lubricants, suppositories and fat-soluble drugs. Cod liver oil and halibut liver oil are used in vitamin A and D therapy, and cod liver oil is also incorporated into ointments for the treatment of wounds and burns. Salmine from salmon sperm and clupeine from herring sperm are used to check haemorrhaging.

Only a minute proportion of the world's plants and animals has been investigated for possible usefulness in medical treatment. Research on compounds from corals, sponges, sea anemones, marine worms, molluscs, sea cucumbers and sea stars is expected to produce better treatments of hypertension, cardiovascular disease and cancers, as well as revealing new antibiotics. Extracts of three sea star species, for example, show promising effectiveness against at least one type of influenza virus.[17]

Since 1960 the US National Cancer Institute has screened some 100,000 extracts from 29,000 plant species. About 3000 of these show potential against cancer, as well as against other diseases. The Institute expects to find that at least five of the compounds discovered will prove sufficiently powerful anti-cancer agents to warrant commercial development.[18]

The evening primrose, which grows wild in North America, is being investigated for its effects on two quite different but equally crippling diseases: schizophrenia and multiple sclerosis. Already 8000 multiple sclerosis sufferers in Europe regularly take oil of evening primrose. Doctors claim that at least 15 per cent of the patients are clearly helped by it and the condition of an additional 15 per cent may be 'marginally improved'.[19]

The quest for better family planning methods is also concentrating on the plant world. This is hardly surprising since the pill, the biggest advance in contraception, itself comes from a wild plant, the Mexican yam.[20] Currently, research centres in Brazil, Hong Kong, South Korea, Sri Lanka, the United Kingdom and the USA are cooperating in a World Health Organization programme to find and test indigenous plants for fertility regulation. Priority is being given to plants that are known to traditional systems of medicine, since they may well be highly effective, would probably have fewer problems of toxicity or harmful side-effects than plants not used traditionally, are most likely to be readily accepted by local populations, and the raw materials for their manufacture are available locally.[21]

Two animals with a new and quite unsuspected importance for medical research are the black bear and the lungfish. The African lungfish is an unprepossessing beast but is remarkable for its capacity to go into suspended animation for long periods. When the shallow lakes and rivers that it lives in go dry, the lungfish (so called because it has lungs as well as gills) buries itself in the mud and goes to sleep, sometimes for as long as two years.

The fish is not really asleep: it simply takes life very easily indeed.

Its heart rate slows and blood pressure drops, oxygen consumption plummets, and the kidney stops work altogether. The lungfish is being studied, appropriately enough, by Dr Alfred P Fishman and his colleagues at the University of Pennsylvania School of Medicine. They hope their work will reveal that the lungfish owes its remarkable capacity to relax to a substance secreted in its blood. Such a substance could be of enormous benefit to medicine, not least in open-heart surgery, where by slowing metabolism it could give surgeons more time to work without risking damage to the patient's brain.[22]

The black bear is another single-minded sleeper. It can sleep for five months, burning 4000 calories each day, without once eating, drinking, urinating or defecating. Dr Ralph Nelson and his colleagues at the Mayo Clinic, Rochester, Minnesota (USA), are seeking a hormone they suspect controls the bear's winter sleep pattern. Discovery of the hormone might offer new ways to treat diseases such as kidney failure. Already, data from the studies have led to the development of an improved high-protein, low-fluid diet for patients with kidney failure.[23]

The battle by plants and animals for space, food and protection from predators and parasites turns every species into a factory for the production of chemical compounds. It would be impossible for us to invent these compounds. Indeed there are so many of them that it may prove impossible just to discover them, and certainly will be if species and habitat destruction persists. All that we have to do is allow our fellow species to survive, and men will have a vast and incredibly variegated ideas bank for as long as they survive.

Wildlife for industry and energy

Many industries besides the food and pharmaceutical industries are based, or depend heavily, on wild plants and animals, and many use them often in quite unsuspected ways. For example, algin from brown seaweeds is used in paints, dyes, building materials (insulation products, sealing compounds, artificial wood), fire-extinguishing foams, paper products, lubricants and coolants in oil drilling, and cosmetics, shampoos and soaps.[24]

New uses based on wild animals are regularly being found. The US company American Cyanamid has produced a light that gives off neither sparks nor heat and can therefore be used under conditions when conventional lighting is extremely dangerous: at mining or industrial accidents, for example, or to illuminate aircraft emergency exit slides. The new light would not have been developed without discovery of how fireflies make the light that gives them their name. The firefly employs a process known as chemoluminescence: the insect secretes two substances, called luciferase and luciferin, which come into contact with each other and in turn with oxygen, react and release energy in the form of light.[25] Recently it was discovered that polar bears, a threatened species, are not white but colourless. Perhaps this discovery is not in itself remarkable, but it looks like pointing the way to two useful technological developments. American scientists have found that polar bear hairs are tiny, translucent pipes that keep the bears warm by funnelling only ultraviolet light through their hollow cores. Polar bears appear white because the insides of the hairs are rough and reflect visible light, just as snowflakes do. Their structure makes polar bear hairs exceptionally efficient heat absorbers, and this could be copied to make warmer cold-weather clothing and far more efficient solar energy collectors.[26]

As for the plant kingdom, industrial attention is turning to those species that can do what petroleum cannot do or can do only at great cost. Prominent among the former is jojoba (pronounced hohoba), a plant that grows wild in the deserts of south-western United States and northern Mexico.

The colourless, odourless oil found in jojoba seeds shares with sperm oil unique properties enabling it to withstand high pressures and temperatures, considered by the automobile industry as essential for the lubrication of automatic transmissions. Efforts to achieve similar properties with mineral oils have failed, so jojoba is the only known substance likely to take the remaining pressure off the sperm whale.

Its other great advantages are that when hydrogenated, jojoba oil forms a hard wax practically identical to spermaceti and carnauba (a very expensive wax scraped from palms growing in Brazil). In addition, jojoba can be cultivated on the reservation land of native Americans in the south-western United States, so that it could help relieve their extreme poverty and even restore some of them to self-sufficiency.[27]

The high and rising costs of petroleum have led to attempts to 'grow' gasoline. Essentially, there are two ways of doing this. One is to grow as much vegetable matter as fast as possible and then to convert it into fuel by a process known as pyrolysis. The vegetable matter, normally wood, is heated in air-free containers to produce several kinds of fuel (methanol, wood oil and gas) and other products (tar, creosote, pitch and acetic acid). Several plant species are suitable for this process, notably sugarcane, cassava and eucalyptus, but one species in particular inspires the enthusiasm of the advocates of bioenergy: *Leucaena leucocophala*, the giant ipilipil. The ipilipil is a native of central America but is widely grown in the Philippines. It is an attractive species for fuel production because it is extremely fast growing, reaching 3.3 metres (almost 11 feet) in six months and almost 15 metres (49 feet) in six years.

The other way of growing gasoline is by growing plants that secrete latex, an emulsion of hydrocarbons and water. The most promising are several species of *Euphorbia* that are rich in hydrocarbon materials. Small-scale experiments suggest that a one hectare plot could produce 2800 to 14,000 litres (740 to 3700 gallons) of oil per year at a cost of $20 per barrel. This method is almost certainly worthwhile now that petroleum prices have risen to that level.[18]

Perhaps the best example of industrial dependence on nature, despite modern technology's capacity for synthesis, is provided by rubber. At one time it was thought that synthetic rubber might replace natural rubber. That idea has been dispelled for good now that the petroleum component of synthetic rubber costs so much. Even then, it was unlikely that synthetic rubber could have replaced natural rubber entirely, since natural rubber has certain unique qualities, such as great elasticity and heat resistance, which are essential for some uses. Truck and bus tyres and automobile radial tyres, for example, use 40 per cent natural rubber, and aircraft tyres must consist almost entirely of natural rubber.[28]

Natural rubber at present makes up 30 per cent of the world rubber market. Although it is a plantation crop, grown chiefly in south-east Asia and west Africa, its long-term viability is likely to depend on wild plants growing in the centre of diversity of the rubber species, ie the tropical rain forests of the Amazon basin.

At the same time other natural sources of rubber are expected to become important. Because the USA now imports almost one million tonnes of natural rubber a year, at a cost of more than $500 million, the US Congress has allocated $60 million for a five-year effort to develop a domestic supply of rubber.

The most promising source seems to be guayule, a shrub that grows in the deserts of north central Mexico and the south-western United States. Guayule plants live for as long as 50 years and flourish in poor, arid soils. All parts of the plant contain a rubber that, when purified, is virtually indistinguishable from natural rubber. In addition, with every ton of rubber, guayule yields half a tonne of valuable resin and 25 kilograms (55 pounds) of hard wax.[28]

The plant kingdom in its diversity is fully equipped to help nations industrialize. Whether industrial societies are as capable of helping the plant kingdom remains to be seen.

Recreation, refreshment and inspiration

Natural areas and wild species supply a multitude of emotional and recreational benefits. National parks and other protected areas attract growing numbers of domestic and foreign visitors. The beauty and behaviour of all kinds of plants and animals delight, inspire and instruct. The sounds, shapes, colours, scents, textures and tastes of the natural world continue to inspire musicians, architects, artists, designers, perfumers and cooks.

The beauty and vivacity of tropical forests could generate an income from tourism quite as substantial. In a few countries, a start has already been made. Luquillo Forest Park in Puerto Rico, for example, attracts half a million visitors a year. The potential is enormous, for there is a surfeit of sights and sounds to delight the visitor. In no other plant community are epiphytes (hanging plants) more abundant or ostentatious. Nowhere else do so many trees exhibit cauliflory, the curious habit of bearing flowers directly on the trunk or larger branches. Only in the tropical forest can the visitor be quite so stimulated yet refreshed by the exuberant inventiveness of so many sounds at once, by turns exquisite, absurd and astonishing.

The life of the seas is a treasure trove of beauty, amusement, emotional stimulus and intellectual challenge, right at the back door of all but 28 of the world's 140 or so countries. Coral reefs have the visual richness of tropical rain forests with the advantage that they can be seen more easily, since the visitor is above or among the action rather than well below it. Fish are the easiest of all wildlife to watch. Molluscs have inspired an enthusiastic following, the miniature architecture of shells making them attractive both to the eye and to the hand.

Whales have become modern totems, inspiring a quasi-religious movement, centred (like so many other cults) in California. A minor industry has grown up around them, consisting of books, records, films and whale watching. Every year 300,000 people watch the migration of the grey whales near San Diego, California. So many spectators now throng to the grey whales' breeding lagoons in Baja,California that they are becoming a threat to the species' well-being. Some 36,000 people visit Peninsula Valdez in Argentina each year to see right whales, and in many other parts of the temperate world crowds flock to sanctuaries and reserves to watch seals.

Wildlife is a major resource base for recreation and tourism. Tourism, largely based on wildlife, is among Kenya's top three foreign exchange earners. In Canada 10 per cent of the population hold hunting licences; in the USA 8 per cent hold hunting licences and 13 per cent hold fishing licences; and in Sweden from 12 to 18 per cent hold fishing licences.[29] Many more people enjoy simply looking at wildlife: in the USA there are about 7 million birdwatchers, 4.5 million wildlife photographers, and almost 27 million nature hikers.[30] For a great many people, too, wildlife is of great symbolic, ritual and cultural importance, enriching their lives emotionally and spiritually.

The bond between people and the natural world is expressed by different cultures in many ways. Nations, provinces, communities and individuals often make symbols of plants and animals. Some most attractive landscapes, such as the rice terraces of the Philippines, are products of a synthesis of culture and nature. People become very attached to places of great natural beauty with important historical or other cultural associations. The cedars of Lebanon, now reduced to mere remnants, have long been lauded by poets, prophets and historians as symbols of strength and eternity.

Wildlife dominates the art, architecture and traditional ceremonies of Papua New Guinea. Animal products are widely used as body ornaments and for cultural exchanges such as bride price. A typical bride price payment might consist of 20 goldlip mother of pearl shells, 3 bailer shells, 15 cowrie shells, 29 pairs of birds of paradise, 12 pesquet parrot headdresses and 10 other feathered headdresses. Birds of paradise have long had a special place in native life, and the plumes are coveted for traditional ceremonies and bride price. The indigenous plume trade is organized essentially to meet a solid economic and cultural demand, deeply interwoven with the habits and traditions of tribes such as the Chimbu.

Crocodile experts from IUCN recently examined Papua New Guinea's crocodile management schemes and were greatly impressed. One expert wrote of the country's unparallelled advantage in having ' "Crocodile People" — people who have a deep understanding of the ways of crocodiles, culturally, spiritually and through everyday contact with the animals. No amount of training can substitute for this natural ability. It is certainly an important national asset.'[31]

The people of Papua New Guinea are not unusual in their love of nature. Indeed the commonly held view among the urban and relatively wealthy that the rural and relatively poor have no appreciation of wildlife is an outrageous fallacy. People who win their subsistence from wild species and natural areas may not demonstrate or march against impending extinctions, and some may help to cause them, but many have an extremely deep involvement with their fellow creatures. For example, according to Madhav Gadgil and V D Vartak, present-day India still abounds in many kinds of nature worship. 'All forms of life', they write, 'from sedges to fig trees, and from crabs to peacocks and tigers continue to be considered sacred and inviolable in relation to a variety of primitive cults.'[32]

The natural world is also essential for scientific innovation. There are estimated to be between 5 million and 10 million different species of plants and animals in the world, of which only about 1.6 million have been named and still fewer have been described.[33] Relatively few can be said to be known completely. These species and the communities they form are living laboratories. Natural areas are essential both for an understanding of fundamental problems of ecology and evolution and as baselines for monitoring changes to other areas together with the consequences of such changes.

The study of plants and animals has launched new scientific disciplines of fields of discovery. Understanding of human genetics has been advanced by understanding the genetics of horseshoe crabs and of fruit flies. Development and reproductive biology began with the study of sea urchin eggs. Natural products also provide essential materials for scientific research. For example, because of its special properties, top-quality agar from red seaweeds is almost uniquely valuable in microbiology as an all-purpose culture medium.

Thus the natural world is our laboratory, playground and temple as well as our larder, medicine chest and store of raw materials. By impoverishing it we only impoverish ourselves and our children.

What should be done?

Preventing the extinction of plant and animal species demands the sound planning and management of land and water uses, supported by specific measures to protect habitats, prevent over-exploitation, and ensure that native species are not harmed by introduced exotic ones. Protected areas such as parks and reserves can preserve more wild species than can zoos and botanical gardens, but to be fully effective both forms of preservation must be part of a programme of rational resource management. This is because it is possible to set

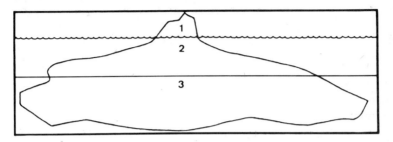

The genetic resource management iceberg. Off site protection (1) can preserve only a small proportion — the 'tip of the iceberg' — of genetic diversity. Protected areas or on site protection (2) can preserve much more, but still very little compared with the potential of the sound planning, allocation and measurement of land and water uses (3). In practice, all three sets of measures are necessary.

aside in protected areas only a small proportion of the earth's surface. If these areas were to become islands in a sea of progressively deteriorating environments, the areas themselves would shrink and support fewer species, being deprived of their support systems. Furthermore, in the case of migratory or wide-ranging animals, protected areas can safeguard only the most vulnerable habitats. Outside those areas, additional measures are necessary.

Where an introduced exotic species is threatening the survival of native species, the introduced species should be eliminated if possible. Given the extreme difficulty of eliminating introduced species, however, every effort should be made to prevent all introductions except those which, before the introduction is made, can be shown to provide economic, social and ecological benefits substantially greater than any costs, and over which adequate control can be exercised. A proposed introduction should be the subject of an environmental assessment, including a full inquiry into the likely and possible ecological effects.

A global programme for protecting habitats

So many species are threatened by habitat destruction and habitats are being wrecked on so wide a front that it is essential to focus on those areas where the reward for a given effort will be greatest. These are the areas where species facing similar problems are concentrated and, therefore, where one set of conservation actions is likely to help many more than one species.

Most plants and land animals threatened by habitat destruction occur in the following environments: freshwaters, wetlands, islands, tropical forests and Mediterranean-type environments. Closer analysis[5] reveals that the key areas for action can be narrowed down more sharply than this. It so happens that conservation of vertebrates (fishes, amphibians, reptiles, birds and mammals) endangered by loss or degradation closely overlap concentrations of vertebrates threatened by the effects of introduced exotic species. More than half the vertebrate species treatened by habitat destruction and 70 per cent of the vertebrate species threatened by the effects of introduced species are concentrated in 10 areas:

— freshwaters in
> North America and Mexico
> west and central Africa
> southern Africa;

— islands in
> Caribbean
> Western Indian Ocean (notably Mauritius, Reunion, Seychelles)
> South Pacific (especially New Caledonia)
> Hawaiian Islands;

— tropical forests in
> south-east Asia
> Madagascar
> South America.

These areas also provide key habitats for a great many threatened plants. In Madagascar, for example, 80 per cent of the country's 10,000 flowering plants are unique to it, as are 575 of its 715 vertebrate species. The yield from conservation efforts in such areas is thus exceptionally high.

Another category of area that must be given priority is that of unusually diverse ecosystems — environments that support a disproportionately large number of species, irrespective of whether they are threatened or not — destruction of which would result in a sudden surge of extinctions. Land areas of exceptional diversity include tropical rain forests (especially those of peninsular Malaysia, Borneo, Celebes, Sumatra, Philippines, New Guinea, central and South America and Madagascar), the tropical dry forests of Madagascar, the Mediterranean-type ecosystems of South Africa and western Australia, and very rich island systems such as New Caledonia and the Hawaiian Islands. Exceptionally diverse marine areas include the coral ecosystems of the Indo-Malay archipelago, the western Pacific, the Red Sea and the Caribbean. Exceptionally diverse freshwater ecosystems include the rivers of west Africa, the lakes of east and central Africa, Lake Baikal in the USSR and the Mississippi drainage of North America.[34]

Some of these areas are more threatened than others. In global terms, tropical rain forests, for example, are at greater risk than coral ecosystems. This does not mean that tropical rain forests should always and as a matter of course be given higher priority than coral reefs. The chances of protective action being completely successful are in general greater for coral ecosystems than for tropical rain forests. The ordering of priorities depends not least on a careful assessment of this factor.

Current programmes to preserve genetic resources tend to be conducted along narrow sectoral lines. They are specific to particular interests: crops, timber trees, livestock, aquaculture or wildlife. This is justifiable in the case of off site preservation in banks, zoos or gardens, since each sector has different needs and therefore requires different collecting programmes. It is not the best approach, however, to on site preservation, given the intense competition for land and water and the relatively tiny proportion of the earth's surface that is likely to be protected with a reasonable degree of long-term security. Genetic resources are a global resource and a cross-sectoral global programme is essential for their on site preservation.

Each sector, therefore, should identify concentrations of the genetic resources most in need of on site preservation. Areas where concentrations overlap should then be selected as priority areas for protection. In some cases the areas may already be protected. In all cases, governments should commit themselves to safeguarding the protected areas. The money for this programme should come not just from governments but also from industries and businesses that directly or indirectly depend on wildlife. Industries and other commercial enterprises based on, or regularly using, particular plant or animal species should sponsor the establishment and maintenance of conservation areas for the preservation of the relevant species, its relatives and varieties. Such areas should be regarded as crop and commodity banks on which the industrial sector concerned can draw for the development of new strains of plant or animal with whatever properties of productivity, pest or disease resistance, responsiveness to different soils and climates, nutritional quality, etc may be required.

Similarly, industries and other businesses that depend on naturally occurring chemical compounds either for raw materials or for product ideas should sponsor the establishment and maintenance of protected areas for the preservation of representative samples of ecosystem types, unique ecosystems, the habitats of unique and of threatened species, and other ecosystems essential for the preservation of genetic diversity. Such areas should be regarded as potential product banks on which the industrial sector concerned (eg pharmaceuticals) can draw for the development of new or improved products.

Every industry should analyse its resource base to determine what living resources it uses and for what purpose, and the extent to which each resource's combination of desired properties, cost and availability is unique to particular plants or animals. Each industry should then work with the governments and the other commercial sectors concerned to ensure that those plants and animals are exploited sustainably, that their genetic diversity is preserved, and that the ecological processes of which they are part are maintained. Such measures would go some way towards ensuring the quality and availability, at reasonable prices, of valuable raw materials.

Stopping over-exploitation

The most promising way of dealing with it on a global scale is through the Convention on International Trade in Endangered Species of Wild Fauna and Flora (CITES). CITES is still very young. Drawn up in Washington in 1973 it did not come into force until July 1975. There were then 10 parties. Now there are 58. This represents a marked advance and one which, in comparison with many other international conventions, represents a very decent growth rate. Yet so long as non-members still greatly outnumber members and so long as the ranks of the former include certain prolific traders in wildlife — Austria, Belgium, Japan among the developed nations, and Colombia, Mexico, Singapore, in the developing world — control will be patchy, even if member countries are performing as they should.

Unfortunately member countries are *not* all performing as they should. Some do not control wildlife products at all. Others do so in a somewhat random and half-hearted manner. Import/export permits and customs returns seldom tally or anything like it. The advertising of 'forbidden' species by private dealers and the selling in shops of 'protected' furs, skins and the like are nothing unusual.

But it would be grossly misleading to give the impression that the convention makes little impact and that members blithely ignore its rules. On the contrary it has demonstrated, especially in recent months, a most heartening ability to wreck the cherished schemes of wildlife racketeers, some of them operating from the sanctuary (or so they may have thought) of non-member states. Growing concern about the plight of endangered species plus a highly alert CITES secretariat have combined to cause countries still outside the convention to react responsibly to events within their domain that would be barred if they were members of CITES.

A further mark of the convention's progress is that offenders are increasingly being arrested and fined (and even occasionally gaoled). Fines, though, remain absurdly light in relation to profits, and on occasions prosecution still has to be brought by some private body because the police consider the matter beneath their attention. In the USA, in November 1978, three companies were fined a total of $87,500 for shipping 2500 alligator skins to tanneries in France. This may seem a large amount, but the shop value of that quantity of skins is $1,000,000, and one of the men involved had already received $140,000 from sales. In Hong Kong, in January 1979, a magistrate imposed the maximum fine $1000 (plus $400 costs) on the Hong Kong Fur Factory Ltd for smuggling 319 cheetah skins from Ethiopia. The magistrate commented that the fine was quite inadequte in relation to the value of the cheetah skins, which were estimated by the fur factory to be worth $40,000 but more objectively valued at 25 times that figure.[10]

The key to the usefulness of CITES is its network of national management authorities and scientific authorities operating in direct communication with each other and the secretariat. The management authority is concerned with the mechanics of trade (such as permits). The scientific authority deals with the biological aspects and must satisfy itself that the issue of a permit will not have a harmful effect on the species concerned. Theoretically the scientific authority has power of veto over the management authority based on its opinion of the status of the species, and therefore provides a mechanism within government's jurisdiction. Effectively, therefore, CITES both regulates international trade in wild species and places an obligation on governments to monitor the status of species.

As member governments in the developing countries often lack the personnel and financial resources to establish and maintain fully operational scientific and management authorities, multilateral and bilateral development assistance agencies should provide assistance on request, and help in the exchange of administrative and scientific experience among trading countries.

Other international agreements

International agreements like CITES can provide a legally binding means of ensuring that the conservation objectives they are concerned with are achieved. Because of their force, they are extremely important for the implementation of the World Conservation Strategy. The stronger agreements need the constant, vigorous support of governments, non-governmental organizations, and international organizations; and the weaker ones need strengthening.

Besides CITES, there are two other strong global conservation agreements: the World Heritage Convention and the Migratory Species Convention. The World Heritage Convention recognizes the obligation of every nation to protect those unique natural and cultural areas which are of such international value that they are part of the heritage of all mankind, and the corresponding obligation of the international community to help them. It is important that all nations join the Convention and contribute generously to the World Heritage Fund set up to help to finance it. The Fund does not reduce the responsibility of each state to protect its unique natural areas, but it does provide a means of ensuring that those areas are not lost because of a local lack of money or skills.

International agreements are the only effective way of protecting animals that cross national boundaries. The Migratory Species Convention, which obliges its members to protect endangered migratory species and to make special agreements for the conservation of those species whose status is 'unfavourable', is therefore very important. The Convention is a new one (it was adopted on 23 June 1979) and several major nations, such as Canada, the USA and the USSR, have not yet signed it.

Their reluctance is due to the agreement covering fish and other migratory species of the seas. Many major fishing nations do not wish to have their fishing activities subject to the control of an international conservation agreement. Yet, of all the migratory animals most in need of improved protection, fish are perhaps the most neglected. It is essential that a great deal of pressure be put on governments to join the Migratory Species Convention and to implement it without delay.

References

1. IUCN (1975) *Red Data Book* IUCN, Gland

2. Lucas, Gren and Synge, Hugh (1978) *The IUCN Plant Red Data Book* IUCN, Gland

3. Smithsonian Institution (1974) *Report on Endangered and Threatened Plant Species of the United States*, presented to the Congress of the United States of America by the secretary, Smithsonian Institution, Washington DC

4. IUCN Threatened Plants Committee (1977) List of rare, threatened and endemic plants in Europe. *Nature and Environment Series* **14** Council of Europe, Strasbourg

5. Allen, Robert and Prescott-Allen, Christine (1978) Threatened vertebrates (second draft). General Assembly Paper GA 78/10 Add 6, IUCN

6. Asibey, Emmanuel O A (1974) Wildlife as a source of protein in Africa south of the Sahara. *Biological Conservation* 6:32-9. And de Vos, Antoon (1977) Game as food. *Unasylva* **29**:2-12

7. Lee, Richard B (1969) Kung bushman subsistence: an input-output analysis. In A P Vayda (ed) *Environment and Cultural Behaviour* University of Texas Press

8. Balinga, V S (1977) Competitive uses of wildlife. *Unasylva* **29**:22-25

9. Anon (23 July 1979) Feathered friends. *Newsweek*. And Anon (1 October 1979) A fly-by-night plot in Australia. *Newsweek*

10. Anon (1979) Endangered Species Meeting. *IUCN Bulletin* **10**:17-24

11. Anon (26 March 1979) Smuggling wildlife. *Newsweek*

12. Rosas, Mateo (1970) *Pescado Blanco (Chirostoma Estor):Su Fomento y Cultivo en Mexico*. Instituto nacional de investigaciones biologico pesqueras/Comision nacional Consultiva de Pesca, Mexico. And Aquaculture development and coordination programme (1979) *Aquaculture Development in Mexico*, report of a review mission 1978, ADCP/MR/79/4. UNDP/FAO

13. Skene, Wayne (5 March 1979) Beef is pricing buffalo right into the market. *Maclean's*

14. Farnsworth, Norman R and Morris, Ralph W (1976) Higher plants: the sleeping giant of drug development. *American Journal of Pharmacy* **146**:45-52

15. UNIDO. (1978) Report of the technical consultation on production of drugs from medicinal plants in developing countries. Lucknow. India. 13-20 March 1978, ID/222 (ID/WG 271/6). UNIDO, Vienna

16. Cohn, Victor (11 August 1977) Drug treatment for a virus is hailed as 'major advance'. *Washington Post*

17. Ruggiere, George D (1976) Drugs from the sea. *Science* **194**:491-497

18. Myers, Norman (1979) *The Sinking Ark* Pergamon

19. Weiler, Meriche. (30 October 1978) The primrose path to health, wealth. *Maclean's*

20. Lewis, Walter H and Elvin-Lewis, Memory P F (1977) *Medical Botany: Plants Affecting Man's Health*. John Wiley. And Morton, Julia F (1977) *Major Medicinal Plants: Botany, Culture and Users* Charles C Thomas

21. Soejarto, D D, Bingel, A S, Slayton, M and Farnsworth, N R (1978) Fertility regulating agents from plants. *Bulletin of the World Health Organization* **56**:343-352

22. Clark, Matt (30 January 1978) Heartening bulletins. *Newsweek*

23. Altman, Lawrence K (23 November 1977) Science wakes up to the hibernating bear. *International Herald Tribune*

24. Naylor, J (1976) Production, trade and utilization of seaweeds and seaweed products. *FAO Fisheries Technical Paper* **159**

25. Lowther, William (23 October 1978) Firefly, firefly burning bright. *Maclean's*

26. Anon (4 December 1978) Furry funnels: are polar bears really white? *Time*

27. Schery, R W (1972) *Plants for Man* Prentice-Hall

28. National Academy of Sciences (1977) *Guayule:An Alternative Source of Rubber* National Academy of Sciences, Washington DC

29. OECD (1979) The state of the environment:an appraisal of economic conditions and trends in OECD countries. ENV/Min (79) 1 OECD, Paris

30. Allen, Durward L (1978) The enjoyment of wildlife. In: Howard P Brokaw (ed) *Wildlife in America*. Council on Environmental Quality, US Fish and Wildlife Service, Forest Service, National Oceanic and Atmospheric Administration, Washington DC

31. IUCN unpublished report

32. Gadgil, Madhav, and Vartak, V D (1976) The sacred groves of the western Ghats of India. *Economic Botany* **30**:152-160

33. Anon (1974) Trends, priorities and needs in systematic and evolutionary biology. *Brittonia* **26**:421-44

34.Goode, Ronald (1974) *The Geography of the Flowering Plants* Longman. And Swift, Camm Churchill (1979) *World Conservation Strategy — Fishes*: a report prepared for the International Union for Conservation of Nature and Natural Resources (Mimeo), IUCN, Gland

Chapter 6

Getting organized : a strategy for conservation

The action described in Chapters 2 to 5 is specific to the more important conservation problems of agricultural systems, forests, the sea and endangered species. They are not concerned with the more fundamental and widespread obstacles to conservation. In this chapter, therefore, are described the priority actions to overcome the six main obstacles to conservation:

1. Absence of conservation at the policy-making level.
2. Lack of environmental planning and of rational use allocation.
3. Poor legislation and organization.
4. Lack of training and of basic information.
5. Lack of support for conservation.
6. Lack of conservation-based rural development.

As well as taking the specific measures that will be discussed later, every country* should prepare its own conservation strategy. Besides helping to focus efforts to overcome the obstacles to conservation, the purpose of national conservation strategies is to accelerate the achievement of conservation objectives by identifying priorities, stimulating action, raising public consciousness and proposing ways of overcoming any apathy or resistance there might be to taking the action needed. Although the planning and execution of conservation strategies is primarily the responsibility of governments, non-governmental organizations should be fully involved to ensure that all the resources available to conservation are deployed coherently and to the full. Indeed in some countries non-governmental organizations may wish to take the initiative.

Anyone preparing a national conservation strategy will need to bear in mind both the general strategic functions mentioned in Chapter 1 and also four strategic principles that are specific to conservation strategies:

1. *Integrate.* The separation of conservation from development together with narrow sectoral approaches to living resource management are at the root of current living resource problems. Many of the priority requirements demand a cross-sectoral, inter-disciplinary approach.
2. *Keep options open.* Our understanding of the dynamics and capacities of many ecosystems, particularly tropical ones, is often insufficient to assure rational use allocation or high quality management. Scientific knowledge of the productive capacities of most tropical ecosystems, as well as of their ability to absorb pollution and other impacts, is generally inadequate. Land and water use, therefore, should be located and managed so that as many options as possible are retained.
3. *Mix cure and prevention.* Current problems are often so severe that it is tempting to concentrate on them alone. Impending problems could be still worse, however, unless early action is taken to prevent them. Strategies for action

---

* 'Country' is here used loosely to mean either nation or sovereign state (for example, Australia, India, Brazil) or province or state (for example, Queensland, Kerala, Minas Gerais) within a nation. Provinces often have considerable responsibilities for living resources and therefore need conservation strategies as much as do nations.

should therefore be a judicious combination of cure and prevention. They should tackle current problems and equip peoples and governments to anticipate and avoid future problems.

4. *Focus on causes as well as symptoms.* When conservation puts itself into the position of dealing only with symptoms it appears unduly negative and obstructive. A late attempt to stop or modify a development, whether successful or not, comes across as anti-development (hence anti-people) even though this is seldom the case. The result is either an outright defeat or, because it generates hostility and misconceptions, a victory that has within it the seeds of future defeats. Furthermore, by the time symptoms appear it is often too late to do anything about them, because many ecologically unsound projects are the results of already fixed policies and part of complex and expensive plans that governments are understandably reluctant to unravel. This said, it is also important not to neglect the symptoms. Although interventions are more effective the earlier in the development process they are made, in practice they are needed at all stages. Moreover, it is sometimes not possible to deal with causes, since many of them are complex and beyond the capabilities of conservation organizations to influence. Action directed at causes generally yields results only over the long term. Symptoms may be so acute that action must be taken immediately.

Conservation and policy making

At the heart of the general failure to achieve the objectives of conservation are the beliefs held by many governments that conservation is a limited, independent sector usually concerned with wildlife or with soil, and that ecological factors are obstacles to development which in some cases may safely be overlooked and in others may be considered simply on a project-by-project basis, not as a matter of policy. These beliefs may not be stated, but they are implicit in the way policies are formulated and in how the plans and programmes derived from those policies are operated.

This narrow interpretation of conservation has at least three important consequences. First, the ecological effects of a particular development policy are seldom anticipated and hence the policy is not adjusted in time to avoid expensive mistakes. Second, those sectors directly concerned with living resources (notably agriculture, forestry, fisheries and wildlife) are often forced to concentrate on exploitation at the expense of conservation, with the result that otherwise renewable resources are squandered and the resource base of future use is undermined. Third (and as a consequence of the first two) other sectors, which though not directly concerned with living resources depend on them at least in part, find their policies frustrated because of a previous lack of conservation. The energy sector's forecasts of the life of a hydroelectric power station, for example, may be completely falsified by poor watershed management.

Even when ecological factors are considered, it is seldom at the critical policy-making stage when the basic pattern of development is often fixed. When ecological considerations are not integrated with policy making, natural resources are often destroyed, economic opportunities are lost, and development projects produce harmful side-effects or fewer benefits or even fail altogether. Although taking account of ecological factors later on, such as when a project comes up for environmental impact assessment, is necessary, it is not enough. By that time adjustments other than cosmetic ones are seldom possible, except at the cost of great social or economic disruption.

For example, attempts to minimize the ecological harm (and hence the social and economic harm) of a dam rarely succeed if ecological factors are considered only at the project stage. By then the dam is a key component of other major projects (such as land clearance, irrigation, and new settlements), themselves essential parts of several sectoral programmes. These programmes are often expressions of social and economic policies from which ecological considerations are entirely absent. Unless ecological considerations influence the development process as much as do social and economic considerations, and unless there is also an explicit policy to achieve conservation objectives, the prospects of avoiding ecological harm and making the best of living natural resources are dim.

Living resource agencies often concentrate on exploitation rather than conservation because of the intense competition within governments for scarce financial resources and the consequent pressure on all sectors to show results that can be directly related to economic performance. Under the circumstances, agencies with the dual task of regulating and promoting resource development are likely to find it difficult to balance the two. This difficulty is exacerbated by the lack of a well defined and generally agreed

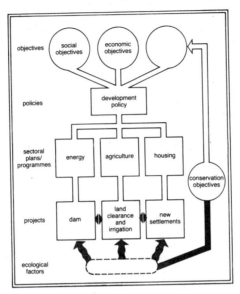

The need to integrate conservation with development: an example. Attempts to minimize the ecological harm (and hence the social and economic harm) of a dam rarely succeed if ecological factors are considered only at the project stage. By then the dam is a key component of other major projects (like land clearance, irrigation, and new settlements), themselves essential parts of several sectoral programmes. These programmes are often expressions of social and economic policies from which ecological considerations are entirely absent. Unless ecological considerations influence the development process along with social and economic considerations — and unless there is also an explicit policy to achieve conservation objectives — the prospects of avoiding ecological harm and of making the best use of living resources are dim. Thus when ecological factors are considered only at the point shown at the bottom of this picture their influence is usually limited or negative. Instead, for development policy to be ecologically as well as economically and socially sound, the empty circle at the top of the picture needs filling as shown.

measure of conservation performance. Economic performance can be measured in terms of gross domestic product (GDP); employment in terms of the percentage of the labour force employed; agricultural, forestry and fisheries production in terms of crop, timber and fish yields and the income derived from them. While such easily measured production may be won at the cost of reducing the resource base, and although conservation can bring real benefits by securing that resource base, the costs and benefits are not readily related.

The lack of an acceptable measure of conservation performance is probably one of the main reasons why central agencies with broad powers to protect the environment nonetheless find it difficult to persuade, for example, the forestry department to exploit forests sustainably or the agricultural department to regulate the use of agricultural chemicals. It also makes it difficult to relate conservation policy goals to other policy goals and therefore to make rational trade-offs between them.

Three measures are required to overcome these problems and to integrate conservation with development at the policy-making level: anticipatory environmental policies; a cross-sectoral conservation policy; and a broader system of national accounting.

Policies aimed at anticipating significant economic, social and ecological events rather than simply reacting to them are becoming increasingly necessary for the achievement of several important policy goals: the satisfaction of basic needs, such as food, clothing, sanitation and shelter; the optimum use of available resources; the provision of a high quality environment; and the prevention of pollution and other forms of environmental degradation. To achieve these goals, policies are required that actively promote human health and well-being. These include the protection of the living resource base, the adoption of resource-conserving settlement patterns, transport systems and modes of trade and consumption, and recycling (including closed-cycle industrial processes). Attempts should also be made to reduce the production, marketing and disposal of products dangerous to the environment, and to make economic use of residual wastes.

Adoption of anticipatory environmental policies poses certain difficulties. By their very nature they require action before damage to the environment has created a demand for it. They also incur the costs of planning, research and preventive action and perhaps those of delays or modifications to particular developments. Yet, in general, these difficulties are heavily outweighed by the advantages. Anticipatory policies enable societies to avoid the high and annually recurring costs of environmental mistakes, which can frustrate development objectives, waste resources, and impair the very capacity for development. Measures to prevent environmental degradation taken at the design stage of products and development projects alike are normally more cost-effective than measures taken once a problem has arisen when they require redesign, restructuring, the banning of a product or the abandonment of a partly completed project.

It is essential that everywhere conservation be conducted on a much more comprehensive basis. This requires all governments to establish a cross-sectoral conservation policy at the highest level, making a public commitment to the achievement of conservation objectives without delay. Not all governments have explicit conservation policies, and the policies that exist tend to be narrowly sectoral. Consequently, opportunities for the joint planning and realization of the conservation requirements of agriculture, forestry, fisheries, wildlife, etc may be overlooked. Indeed, the policies of the sectors concerned may conflict. Similarly, the interests of sectors not usually thought of as deriving benefits from living resource conservation may be neglected. Conservation has an important contribution to make to the successful operation of a great many government programmes, including human settlements, health, agriculture, fisheries and industry. It can, for example, help a health programme not only by promoting a healthier environment and safeguarding water supplies but also by preserving the genetic resources needed for the production of medicines. In addition, as a matter of policy, the primary mission of government agencies directly concerned with living resources should be conservation. The need for food, fuel and fibre and other natural products, as well as for foreign exchange, may tempt living resource managers into encouraging or permitting over-exploitation of the resources in question or the undermining of the ecological processes and genetic diversity on which they depend. This is highly likely if policy goals are concerned mainly with production and only incidentally with maintenance.

The costs of conservation, as well as of measures to improve human welfare in other ways, may often appear to outweigh the benefits, since the costs are entirely calculable in money while the benefits are not. This is not a deficiency of conservation, nor of economics, but is the result of extending the use of economic tools to policy areas where they are not applicable. In evaluating the costs and benefits of conservation (and of many other human endeavours), it is useful to distinguish four kinds of value:

— *economic* or *market* value, calculable in money terms;
— *useful*, expressed as utility for persons or welfare for society;

— *intrinsic*, valued without reference to usefulness or to things that can be bought in its place;

— *symbolic*, standing for something else that is valued, usually something abstract (like conservation or development).[1]

Thus a whale may be of economic value to commercial whalers, of useful value to subsistence hunters, of intrinsic value to other people for its beauty, and of symbolic value to still others as a symbol of conservation. Economic and useful values can be quantified, in terms of money and in terms of whatever measure is appropriate (for example, weight or protein in the case of meat) respectively. Useful values can sometimes also be quantified without distortion in terms of money, but by no means always. Intrinsic and symbolic values can scarcely ever be quantified without making a mockery of them.

It is wise to distinguish carefully between each of these kinds of value. Many proposed public works, for example, have an unstated symbolic value (symbolizing 'development' or 'progress') and great efforts may be made to inflate estimates of the economic benefits and deflate those of the costs in order to accommodate the project's symbolic worth. When cost-benefit analyses attempt to put a price on items of useful, intrinsic or symbolic value, the assumptions behind such price fixing should be made explicit so that the policy maker can decide what weight to give the various factors in the analysis. Also, for adequate account to be taken of the costs of destroying or damaging living resources and of the benefits of conserving them, non-economic indicators of conservation performance should be selected for inclusion in national accounting systems. This is easier said than done, but possible indicators are outlined below.

1. Extent of most suitable agricultural land that has not been lost to non-agricultural activities or degraded by poor farming practices.
2. Silt load of rivers as a proportion of the size of the river basin (as a measure of erosion).
3. Proportion of unique species and of unique varieties of domesticated plants and animals whose survival is secured.
4. Proportion of resource ecosystems and species which are being exploited sustainably.

Environmental planning and rational use allocation

Environmental planning and the allocation of uses on the basis of planning are essential if optimum use is to be made of available resources. Without them, the prospects of conservation and sustainable development will be impaired, sometimes permanently. For example, dams may be silted so that they drown and destroy highly productive land or important areas of genetic diversity. Pollution emission standards may be set so low that acid rain reduces the productivity of forests and freshwaters, or pathogens and heavy metals contaminate food (such as shellfish) rendering it unmarketable or, if it is marketed, directly damaging human health. Industries and settlements may be built on the best farmland or on land 'reclaimed' from coastal wetlands, thus reducing the productivity of agriculture and fisheries.

To ensure that environmental planning is as sound as possible, an integrated method of land and water evaluation is needed. Many countries already evaluate land for different uses. For example, the US Soil Conservation Service assesses land according to a detailed classification system. This takes account of soil types, the slope and drainage of the land, the rockiness of the soil and its susceptibility to erosion, and similar factors. Like most land capability assessments, it is thus primarily concerned with the capability of land for agriculture and forestry.

What is now needed is an extension of this type of assessment. Land areas should be evaluated not only for their agricultural capabilities but also for any other qualities that make them important for conservation. These include watershed protection; the provision of critical habitats (for breeding, sheltering young, feeding, resting) for threatened, unique or culturally and economically important species; and areas important for the preservation of genetic diversity (such as unique areas, representative samples of different types of area, and areas rich in species or in important varieties). At the same time, freshwater and marine areas — including important coastal wetlands and shallows, genetically rich areas, areas that support actual or potential fisheries, and critical habitats — should also be evaluated.

In this way all of the significant living resource aspects of a country can be evaluated rather than just a somewhat arbitrary selection of them. This is particularly important since often one form of living resource use may conflict with another. For example, an exclusively agricultural assessment may regard a wetland as being a fine candidate for conversion to farmland, thereby depriving a valuable fishery of essential support.

Ecosystem evaluations (EEs) can vary in detail depending on their purpose. For policy makers EEs need only be at the level of a reconnaissance: a broad inventory of ecosystems and their characteristics at national and sub-national scales, with evaluation that is largely qualitative. EEs at this level are integrating mechanisms. They enable policy makers to take account of ecological, social and economic criteria simultaneously and thus to make informed choices before resources are irrevocably committed. They can suggest those development opportunities likely to be both productive and sustainable, and show where trade-offs between one policy and another may be expected to be large or small. If all policies were adjusted at this point, many resource conflicts could be minimized, and others resolved without social or economic disruption.

EEs will need to be supplemented by more detailed environmental impact assessments (EIAs) of proposed policies, laws, programmes and projects. EIAs are an indispensable means of scrutinizing proposed actions for their likely ecological and other consequences. Governments should ensure that all major developments — including those (such as aid projects) they take abroad and actions with effects on other countries (for example, the damming of a river that flows into another country, or the construction of a power plant that might pollute another country's air) — are assessed thoroughly for their environmental impact. This also requires the examination of alternatives to the proposal assessed and a review of all such assessments by an independent body.

EEs, supplemented by EIAs, will provide the policy maker with an

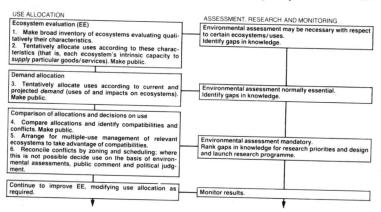

The relationship between the allocation of land and water uses and assessment, research and monitoring.

130

analysis of the capacity of land and water areas to supply particular goods and services (or fulfil particular functions). In order to make optimum use of the identified supply characteristics of these areas, it is recommended that the procedure for allocating uses be conducted roughly as follows. First, uses should be allocated tentatively according to their compatibility with the areas' *supply* characteristics as determined by EEs. Areas with potential for multiple use should be identified and such uses specified. Second, the current and projected pattern of *demand* on these areas, as reflected by current use, should be analysed. Here, demand equals present uses of, plus impacts on, the areas. Current uses of each area should be identified and projected increases and changes in demand indicated. At this stage demand for non-living resources (construction materials, minerals, oil, gas, space for roads and buildings) as well as the effects of energy consumption and settlement patterns should be included. Uses should then be allocated tentatively a second time, according to this analysis of present and projected demand. Finally, the results of allocation by supply characteristics and of allocation by demand characteristics should be compared to reveal conflicts and compatibilities between the two. Conflicts can often be avoided by zoning, but if this is not possible their resolution will be a matter of political judgement.

Legislation, organization, training and basic information

Policies are of little value unless there is a capacity to implement them. This may seem obvious enough, but many countries fail to implement their living resource policies (however good they may be) because legislation, organization, training and information are inadequate. This failure is one of the biggest obstacles to the achievement of conservation.

In many countries legislation concerning living resources is marred by gaps, duplication and even conflicts. A still more common and especially serious problem is the failure to implement laws and regulations whatever their quality. Sometimes lack of implementation is due to the law being so stringent that people must flout it to survive. Generally, however, it is because the law implies a governmental commitment and infrastructure that simply do not exist. Legislation may, for example, authorize the sale of pesticides only upon a written affidavit that the pesticide has been tested, yet the facilities for testing may be inadequate. Often when budgets are entirely inadequate for enforcement, penalties are weak and jurisdictional conflicts between agencies or between central government and local government prevent the law from being implemented.

The most widespread reason for failure of implementation is a lack of trained personnel. In some African countries the lack of environmental lawyers means that out-of-date colonial laws are not revised or another country's legislation is duplicated without being adapted to local conditions. Lack of trained staff is also the major constraint on the implementation of other conservation measures.

Some countries need people trained in living resource management, such as foresters and watershed managers. Indonesia, for example, currently has only 400 foresters, or one forester per 3000 square kilometres of forest (fewer than one per timber concession).[2] The list of scientists and professionals needed by developing countries is long: ecologists, geologists, hydrologists, public health engineers, environmental economists, environmental planners and so on. Even where professional staff are available there is an acute shortage of technicians. Scientists, for example, may find themselves having to maintain their own equipment. Sometimes the shortage of technicians is exacerbated by the shortage of professionals, because successful trainee technicians may decide to continue their education so that they can achieve the higher status and salaries of the professions.

The acute lack of trained personnel in developing countries is the result of three factors: inadequate training facilities; low salaries (notably in relation to the private sector); and poor administrative organization. What foresters there are may be located only in national and provincial capitals. Because field staff are paid even less than headquarters staff, and because of the hardship of life in the field, more than half the trained foresters in Thailand work in Bangkok.[3]

Also because of lack of money and trained personnel, many developing countries suffer from inadequate information. Generally this is because the countries' data gathering capabilities are weak, but even when they are satisfactory information flow is hampered by poor data retrieval and distribution systems. As a result of such deficiencies countries lack such basic information as estimates of the extent of forest cover and rates of its removal, aquatic pollution levels and assimilative capacities, and species inventories for protected areas.

Comprehensive air and water monitoring systems are so expensive and sophisticated that only developed countries can afford them.

Not enough is known about the dynamics of tropical ecosystems to develop less expensive but equally reliable systems using species as indicators of ecosystem health. The level of applied research on ecosystems and their modification needs to be stepped up considerably if policy makers are to be given better advice on such matters as the extent to which coastal wetlands can be modified, the pollution absorption capacities of freshwaters, and the most favourable cropping patterns for integrated pest control.

Although a great deal is known about many species and ecosystems, what we know about the biosphere is less than what we do not know. The dynamics and relationships of many important ecosystems are little understood. It is therefore seldom possible to predict accurately — at least not in a way that might be useful to a policy maker — the effects of human actions on a great many ecosystems without special and often lengthy research. The same generalization applies to determining sustainable yields from multi-species fisheries. Such lack of knowledge often causes difficulties between policy makers and resource managers on the one hand and the ecologists and other scientists that advise them on the other. The former expect clear and precise advice; the latter cannot avoid stressing the real and important uncertainties that exist.

Governments and resource users are scarcely ever in a position to defer action pending the outcome of a protracted research pro-gramme. Yet action based on inadequate knowledge carries a grave risk that it will fail or be unnecessarily destructive. Unacceptable consequences of lack of knowledge are best avoided or alleviated by good planning and management, so that development activities can be so located and conducted that risk is reduced. At the same time management needs to be more research-orientated and research more management-orientated so that the most urgently required knowledge is generated more quickly.

Every country should review the organization and funding of government agencies with responsibilities for living resources, together with the legislative provisions governing actions affecting living resources. They should take the necessary steps, including changes in legislation, to ensure that conservation policies are implemented and that the agencies concerned have the resources and staff to carry out promptly and fully ecosystem evaluations, environ-mental impact assessments and any other measure required for the conservation of living resources. The following general principles should form the basis for organization within government to achieve conservation:

1. The different agencies with responsibilities for living resources should have clear mandates and such mandates should specify conservation.
2. There should be a permanent mechanism for joint consultation on and coordination of both the formulation and the implementation of policies.
3. Each agency should be required by statute to disclose and explain its positions to the public.
4. Policies and decisions should be implemented. Sufficient financial and other resources should be provided to make this possible.
5. The more limited the availability of trained planners and managers the more important it is to avoid dispersing them among agencies with narrow mandates and conflicting aims.
6. The policies, plans and programmes of the central, provincial and local governments of a country should be closely coordinated. Jurisdictions should be clearly defined, and there should be a mechanism for allocating as yet unforeseen responsibilities.

Every country should also review the capacities of its universities and other centres of higher education to train professionals and technicians in the expertise and skills necessary for planning and managing living resources. National and regional training facilities should be strengthened as appropriate. To encourage recruitment at the technical level it may be necessary to provide professional recognition to technicians. Where disparities between private sector and public sector salaries accentuate the shortage of trained personnel, public sector salaries should be increased. Similarly, the salaries of field personnel should be at least as high as those of headquarters staff, and indeed may need to be higher to compensate for poor conditions.

Support for conservation

Ultimately, living resources are being destroyed because people do not see that it is in their interests not to destroy them. The benefits from natural ecosystems and their component plants and animals are regarded by all but a few as trivial and dispensable compared with the benefits to be got from those activities that entail their destruction or degradation.

The most effective way of convincing people of the merits of

Trainees at the Garoua College of Wildlife Management, Cameroon.

conservation is to enable them to participate in the decisions concerning living resources. Local community involvement and consultation and other forms of public participation in planning, decision making and management are valuable means of testing and integrating economic, social and ecological objectives. They also provide a safeguard against poorly considered decisions and an indispensable means of educating the public in the importance and problems of conservation, and policy makers, planners and managers in the concerns of the public. Participation tends to build public confidence and improve the public's understanding of management objectives; and it provides additional data for planners and policy makers.

If the users of living resources (farmers, fishers, foresters, industries based on living resources, recreational users, etc) are unaware of the need to conserve the resources they are using, an education campaign should be prepared for them. This also applies to other groups that may have an impact on living resources, if they are unaware of the need to manage their activities in ways that are as compatible as possible with conservation. Similarly, if government does not recognize the need to meet the conservation requirements concerned, special efforts will be needed to direct information on the importance of such requirement to the appropriate legislators and decision makers.

Advantage should be taken of circumstances in which legislators, decision makers and others may be induced to pursue policies of conservation. Some sets of favourable circumstances are outlined below.

1. When pro-conservation decisions are evidently the most profitable.
2. When pro-conservation decisions are an effective way of achieving other policy objectives.
3. If political leaders are personally convinced that conservation policies are the right course to pursue.
4. If the electorate supports conservation policies and makes it clear that it will vote for those policies.
5. If influential groups within the country are educated in and committed to conservation policies.

Organizers of education programmes should determine the main target groups of the programmes, define precise programme objectives, and select the media and techniques that are most effective with the target groups. The techniques and materials used should be regularly evaluated against the stated objectives. The most important target groups are:

— governments and legislators;
— development practitioners, industry and commerce, and trades unions;
— professional bodies and special interest groups; communities most affected by conservation projects; schoolchildren and students.

Ultimately the behaviour of entire societies towards the biosphere must be transformed if the achievement of conservation objectives is to be assured. A new ethic, embracing plants and animals as well as people, is required for human societies to live in harmony with the natural world. The long-term task of environmental education is the fostering or reinforcement of attitudes and behaviour compatible with this new ethic.

Conservation-based rural development

A great many rural people, especially in developing countries, are extremely poor, some 1200 million people being classified by the United Nations as 'seriously poor' (of whom almost 800 million are 'destitute') with 500 million suffering from malnutrition.[4] In their effort to satisfy their needs for food and fuel, the rural poor strip the land of trees and shrubs for firewood, clear steep and unstable slopes for cultivation, overgraze pastures, and overhunt and overfish the local wildlife. As a result the daily survival decisions of the poor and hungry disrupt their own life-support systems, impair ecological processes and destroy genetic and other renewable resources just as surely as do too many of the development decisions of the rich and powerful in government and industry. The rural communities responsible for this destruction seldom need to be told it is a mistake. They are made acutely aware of it by a constant and increasing lack of food, fuel, and other necessities. But such communities need to be equipped to win their livelihoods using conservationist methods. Yet development is passing them by.

Rural people, because they are dispersed over very wide areas, are less advantageously placed than their urban compatriots to bring their problems to the attention of government. For the same reason, their problems are less amenable to the kinds of development that governments with a narrow tax base, inadequate institutions, poor delivery of services to rural areas and a vociferous urban population usually initiate. It is ostensibly easier, and certainly more visible, to plan, finance and manage a few large-scale projects than to promote and oversee many village-scale projects. Even though it is still easier to obtain international finance for big developments, such as pulp mills, dams, or international airports, their planning and management leave much to be desired. They are often short-lived or marred by harmful side-effects, and they yield few benefits to the rural poor.

Furthermore, developments that do bring real benefits, such as improved health services, better veterinary services, new wells, and higher yielding crop varieties, also bring additional changes to a situation that is already changing rapidly because of sheer pressure of numbers. But such developments come separately and not as part of a coordinated rural development programme, and they often end up by worsening problems of the rural poor. For example, improved veterinary care, new wells and the opening up of previously uninhabitable land by the eradication or control of diseases such as trypanosomiasis have enabled pastoralists to increase their livestock numbers and provided them with new areas of grazing land in part compensation for areas lost to farmers. However, where these developments have not been accompanied by effective provisions for better pasture management, the eventual result is usually heavy overgrazing and often irreversible soil degradation. Similarly, the change from shifting cultivation to settled arable farming, which is essential when the cultivation/fallow cycle becomes unstable and pressure on soil and vegetation increases, can cause still greater erosion unless farmers are equipped to apply the necessary soil conservation measures. In rural development, as in development generally, the narrow sectoral approach is almost invariably self-defeating.

Rural communities need help to conserve their living resources as the essential basis of the development without which they cannot survive. If soil and vegetation need to be restored, they must be given a respite from intensive use. This requires integrated action to reduce livestock numbers (possibly through price supports that encourage sale to market), increase the efficiency of food production on nearby farms, employ local people in replanting and reseeding schemes, and provide alternative settlement areas and alternative sources of water and fuel and other services (health, education, job training, etc).

Protected areas and other conservation measures may restrict access to fuel, food, forage and other products. Compensatory measures, including pasture improvement, the establishment of fuelwood plantations and the provision of credit or alternative food, fuel or fibre, will then be needed. If the measures concerned take time to bear fruit they must be supplemented by measures bringing immediate benefits. For example, if a protected area or a watershed forest is threatened by wood-cutting for fuel, it will be necessary not only to establish a fuelwood plantation but also to provide an alternative source of fuel that can be used at once. It would also be prudent to provide the community concerned with the means of conserving fuel supplies, such as more efficient cookers.

If land is eroding so rapidly that it must be retired, there is seldom any alternative to the generally difficult tasks of resettling the farmers concerned elsewhere or of absorbing them into other sectors of the economy. It is desirable, therefore, to prevent situations where land retirement is the only solution, by promoting systems of

A Masai herdsman and his cattle at a water hole in Amboseli, Kenya. The perennial waters of this national park are vital to all the region's animal life during the dry seasons. (Photo: Robert C Milne).

production adapted to ecological conditions, in which modern technology and techniques are integrated with traditional systems of resource management. This is particularly important for communities whose shifting cultivation practices have become unstable because the rising population demands more intensive production than the soil can support without considerable improvement.

The techniques and inputs of sustainable permanent cropping, such as fertilizers, improved seed, and soil conservation measures, are usually beyond the economic means of poor farmers. But it is possible to shorten the fallow period of shifting cultivation gradually through mixed cropping practices, the limited use of inorganic fertilizers, and recycling organic materials. It is also possible to improve the efficiency of the fallow period by substituting the natural cover with cover crops, some of which (pasture for livestock in mixed agri-pastoral systems and tree crops in mixed agrisilvicultural systems) can be used economically.

Many tropical soils quickly lose their fertility. Traditional systems of shifting cultivation restored fertility by leaving the land fallow for long periods, but under continuous cropping fertilizers are indispensable. Manufactured fertilizers are beyond the means of many developing country farmers because of their high costs, low prices for farm products, shortage of credit and a lack of fertilizer supplies at national or local level. The estimated 113 million tonnes of plant nutrients that are potentiallly available to developing countries from human and livestock wastes and from crop residues should, therefore, as far as possible be used to fertilize the land.[5] The use of organic wastes as plant nutrients and soil restorers can be combined with the production of biogas (methane). This process eases the problems of storing and delivering organic wastes, reduces the loss of organic matter through decomposition and provides gas for domestic uses.

For conservation-based rural development to be successful, there will need to be more research into sustainable systems of producing food and other goods from the rural sector. Moreover training and incentives programmes will have to be instituted to encourage and equip rural communities to adopt those systems that are known to work now. An indispensable incentive and ultimately the one most likely to work is demonstration within the communities concerned that the new systems provide a higher quality of life using the resources to hand.

Many traditional methods of living resource management, however, are worth retaining or reviving, either in their original or in modified forms. For example, field experiments with traditional cropping systems in various parts of the world have demonstrated that many of these systems bring high yields, conserve nutrients and moisture, and suppress pests.[6] The efficiency of traditional cropping systems can often be increased not by introducing completely different ones but by identifying those elements which could be improved and making the appropriate improvement. For example, Indonesian combinations of corn and rice have been shown to be not only resistant to pests but also more responsive than monocultures to applications of nitrogen fertilizer.[6] The original strategy of the so-called 'green revolution' of replacing tropical polycultures (growing a number of crops together) with temperate-style monocultures is increasingly being reversed. The new strategy is to retain the most productive elements of tropical polycultures and improve the remainder.

The quickest and speediest way of meeting the needs of the needy majority is through the use of resources to hand. The poor do not regard living resources as superfluous or as a fad of the rich. For them they are absolutely essential. When they destroy those resources by farming unsuitable land, gathering too much wood, or overhunting and overfishing local wildlife, it is not through greed or irresponsibility, nor from a feeling that there is plenty more where it came from, nor in many cases from ignorance. It is from sheer desperation.

The poor sometimes take into their own hands the protection of the natural areas on which their fate hangs. Hundreds of Indian villagers in the Himalayas have decided that the best way to save their trees is to hug them. They have started what they call Chipko Andolan, the hugging movement. They fling their arms around trees that are about to be felled, and, in Gandhian style, non-violently prevent the logging contractors from working. The Chipko people want the forests restored to their own use because their subsistence economy depends on the forests. They also want the watershed to be protected. Since the forests were opened to commercial exploitation, felling has been excessive and has produced predictable results: erosion, siltation of rivers and floods.

The special problems of tribal minorities

A surprisingly large number of people still live in tribal groups, feeding themselves and meeting most of their other needs directly from hunting, fishing, plant gathering or farming. Their role in the cash economies that surround them is modest, although increasingly they are being drawn into them. But the special needs of tribal minorities are often overlooked. Development goes ahead, ostensibly to benefit all people, with scarcely any thought that it might be destroying both their means of survival and their cultures.

In Africa, Asia and South America, the drowning of land by dams and the felling of forests for commercial timber production or for cattle ranching too often displace small farming communities. Their members have to make do with less, become casual wage earners or drift to the cities.

In Alaska, the over-exploitation of the few Arctic resources considered profitable (whales, seals, salmon, etc) has forced many self-sufficient Inuit (Eskimos) to depend, at least in part, on welfare. Now oil and gas development threatens to undermine their subsistence base entirely. Such development will pollute or degrade the habitats of fish and game; stimulate ancillary developments, such as roads, pipelines and settlements, which disturb wildlife and may destroy the environments on which it depends; and attract large numbers of people, many of whom take up hunting and fishing for sport and so compete with the Inuit for their livelihood (the number of sport fishing licences rose from 4450 in 1940 to 124,000 in 1973).

Even modest and well-meaning developments can be devastating. The Botswana Government is trying to expand the national cattle herd and increase beef export revenues. Areas of the Kalahari that once supported no cattle at all, or a few infrequently, are now being ranched or opened up to Tswana herdsmen. Cattle, however, are not well adapted to semi-arid conditions. Unlike native animals (such as the great antelopes), they have to drink every other day, crowding around watering points and overgrazing limited areas. They break up the fragile sand surface, beginning a probably irreversible process of dune formation and invasion by woody plants and non-nutritious grasses, useless to cattle and game alike. The sinking of boreholes enables cattle to compete with game in areas they would not otherwise enter, and upsets the delicate water balance of the desert by allowing water to be consumed more quickly than it can be replenished.

The once lush areas of eastern Botswana are now desert because of uncontrolled grazing. The drier parts of the Kalahari proper are much less able to withstand this sort of pressure. It might be possible to ranch indigenous game animals, but to extend the area of cattle production is ecological and economic suicide. By thus transforming semi-desert into true desert, even hunting and gathering are rendered impossible, and the survival and relative well-being of thousands of people imperilled.

Most tribal minorities have ceased to be self-sufficient. With the centralization of their communities into conventional settlements, native Alaskans need motor-boats and snow machines to reach those parts of their hunting territories in which formerly they lived. The San hunter-gatherers of the Kalahari are beginning to want to learn how to read and write so that they can meet the pressures of the cash economy with at least some of its weapons. The small farmers of the tropical forests need steel implements and adequate health services. New diseases demand new cures and altered environments require changes in the technologies of their exploitation.

Planning and policy making for tribal peoples the world over assume for them the Hobson's choice of neglect on the one hand or proletariatization on the other, of *total* participation in either the subsistence economy or the cash economy. Neither alternative is possible nor desirable in the foreseeable future, nor (as far as they have been consulted) does either seem to be desired by the peoples themselves.

If tribal minorities are forced to abandon the bulk of their subsistence activities, they will be thrust into the limbo of poverty, which few of them suffered before contact with the cash economy. The Yupik Inuit's average income per person per year is $800. The US Fish and Wildlife Service has estimated that if they had to buy the equivalent of the food they catch, each of them would need an additional $2200 a year. The total cost of replacing the subsistence foods of Alaska's Yukon-Kuskokwin Delta region alone would be $300 million. There are almost 40,000 other Eskimos, Aleuts and Indians elsewhere in Alaska who still depend to a substantial degree on fishing, hunting and plant gathering.

Dollars are an inadequate measure of the loss to subsistence peoples of their own food resources. Food from shops and markets is subject to inflation; subsistence food is not. The subsistence diet is more varied and nourishing than the poor commercial diet that generally replaces it. The traditional diet of the San is one of the most protein-rich in the world, averaging 93.1 grams per person per day (the average daily *per capita* intake in, for example, Britain is 87.5 grams). In remote areas like most of Alaska, the Kalahari and many tropical forest regions, fresh food is almost impossible to buy. Finally, many subsistence peoples strongly prefer the food they provide for themselves to food bought in shops.

San who have stopped hunting and gathering have become miserably indigent hangers-on to Botswana's semi-capitalist, semi-feudal cattle enterprises. Tropical farmers deprived of their subsistence have joined the flood of migrants to the towns, there to suffer a standard of living much lower than the one they knew at home.

Tribal people's prospects of prosperity depend not on their being pushed into the developmental chasm between subsistence and the cash economy but on their being allowed to create a quite different economy, one which combines elements of the two. Where they have been permitted to articulate their own vision of the future, this is what the tribal minorities themselves seem to desire. The Yupik have specifically rejected both a return to a life entirely removed from the cash economy and its wholesale espousal. They would like to develop a combination of the two: to continue to get the bulk of their food by subsistence means, but to participate in commercial life to the extent

143

that they can earn enough money to buy ammunition, fishing gear, fuel, some clothing and furnishings. They do not want oil and gas exploitation to be halted, but slowed down and extended over many more years than is presently envisaged. They ask that habitats critical for subsistence be closed to destructive forms of development, and that elsewhere strict environmental standards be enforced. But they do not demand that development be checked entirely. For them it is the best of both worlds, or no world at all.

References

1. I am grateful to Lord Ashby for this classification. See Ashby, Eric (1978) *Reconciling Man with the Environment* Oxford University Press

2. Myers, Norman (1979) *The Sinking Ark* Pergamon

3. US Agency for International Development (1979) Environmental and natural resources management in developing countries: a report to Congress, Volume 1: Report. USAID, Department of State, Washington DC

4. ILO (1972) *Employment, Growth and Basic Needs* ILO, Geneva. And World Bank (1978) *World Development Report* World Bank, Washington DC

5. FAO (1978) *The State of Food and Agriculture 1977* FAO, Rome

6. International Rice Research Institute (1974) *Annual Report for 1973* IRRI, Los Banos

Chapter 7
Implementing the strategy

Paper strategies save only paper tigers. Needless to say, the Strategy will only be of use if it is actually carried out and achieves results. How will this be done? And who will do it?

At the international level, the five organizations most closely involved in the Strategy's preparation (International Union for Conservation of Nature and Natural Resources, United Nations Environment Programme, World Wildlife Fund, Food and Agriculture Organization of the United Nations, and United Nations Educational, Scientific and Cultural Organization) can be expected to work closely together to promote the Strategy's implementation. They will concentrate on stimulating governments to take the action recommended in previous chapters, and within the limits of their resources they will give what help is needed to do this. For its part, IUCN will monitor implementation as closely as possible, publishing regular reports, including a full progress report every three years. This will cover what governments and organizations are doing to implement the Strategy, whether what they are doing is likely to alleviate the problem or achieve the objective concerned, and at later stages the extent to which the three conservation objectives have been achieved.

Governments and voluntary organizations have already started to take action in response to the Strategy. By January 1980 New Zealand and the Soviet Union had started work on national conservation strategies. The Brazilian government was also contemplating the preparation of a national conservation strategy, and was discussing it with Brazilian conservation organizations. In Norway, a special commission chaired by the Chairman of the Norwegian Parliament was examining the status of living resource conservation in Norway. The commission had drawn on the Strategy to help it in its work. India's next economic plan has a chapter on conservation for the first time ever, an encouraging step forward stimulated in large part by the World Conservation Strategy.

National conservation action must be promoted systematically. There are several ways this can be done, but the Strategy opts for cooperative programmes involving governments, international organizations and the private sector. These programmes should have a clear focus, concentrating either on a theme (such as tropical forests or desertification) or a region. Regional strategies are a particularly useful way of stimulating national action, of helping to solve problems common to more than one country, and of advancing the conservation of shared living resources (such as a river basin or sea shared by two or more nations or a species that migrates from one country to another).

Each regional strategy should aim for at least four results:

— agreements on the joint conservation of shared living resources;
— model examples of how common problems can be tackled successfully;
— joint organizations where appropriate and where more cost-effective than several national organizations (for example, for training, for research and monitoring, or for the management of shared living resources);
— improved information for national decision making.

Each 'region' should be an ecological unit in which by definition many of the living resources will be shared. Obvious examples, and priority candidates for regional strategies, are international river basins and seas.

Perhaps the most important form of international action is the development of international conservation law and of the means to implement it. Strong international conventions or agreements provide a legally binding means of ensuring the conservation of those living resources that cannot be conserved by national legislation alone. International law also provides an often essential and always valuable set of self-imposed obligations on national behaviour, an indispensable tool in an interdependent world.

Law, however, is seldom enough. Many governments may have the will to conserve but lack the means. It is therefore essential not only that the amount of development assistance going to developing countries be raised but also that a very much greater proportion of it be spent on integrating conservation and development.

The funds spent by multilateral and bilateral development assistance agencies (more than $27,000 million in 1976)[1] can do a great deal towards restoring the environment, tackling environmentally induced poverty, and enabling countries to make the best use of their resources, if the projects they support are environmentally sound. These agencies should make every effort to:

1. Direct funds to reforestation, the restoration of degraded environments, and the protection of watersheds, of mangroves and other critical habitats for marine resources, and of genetic resources essential for development.
2. Assess all projects for their ecological implications and ensure that they are ecologically sound.
3. Assist governments to design ecologically appropriate policies and to establish and maintain effective conservation laws and organizations.

Assistance should be made available to enable requesting nations to develop the capacity to carry out ecosystem evaluations and environmental assessments, and to implement cross-sectoral conservation policies through appropriate legislation, training and organization. Development agencies should assist governments to establish the laws, institutions and procedures to enable them to conserve their country's living resources. Developing industries based wholly or partly on living resources should be encouraged and equipped to ensure that the resources are exploited sustainably and that the genetic diversity on which ultimately they depend is preserved. Development aid agencies have a special responsibility to help — through the provision of appropriate advice and technical assistance — the recipient nation to ensure that financial assistance makes the best use of the living resources it is likely to affect. They should endeavour to ensure that:

— the proposed development is compatible with the recipient country's national conservation policy and strategy (if they exist);
— the proposed development is the most appropriate response to the capabilities of the ecosystems concerned;
— as far as possible the potential of the ecosystems concerned is retained;
— an environmental assessment is carried out.

Nations lacking the capacity to carry out ecosystem evaluations or environmental impact assessments or lacking adequate conservation laws, means of enforcing them, or organizations to effect the full range of required conservation measures should seek multilateral or bilateral assistance to acquire it. If necessary, they should also seek assistance for the preparation of a conservation strategy.

Conservation is not the responsibility of governments alone. There is a great deal that the private sector can do. The three main things conservation organizations should do are:

1. Switch much of their effort to influencing policies rather than reacting to the results of such policies. When conservation is put into the position of *resisting* rather than *guiding* development, it is either ignored or, if it is successful, the effects are often expensive, socially divisive, and ultimately counter-productive.
2. Speed the establishment and implementation of strong conservation laws and institutions, for example by promoting the adoption of international agreements that require the establishment of improvement of conservation organization (such as the scientific and management authorities of CITES) and encouraging countries to join them and to implement them fully.
3. Mount a sustained public education drive directed primarily at governments, the business community, organized labour and the professions, aimed at showing the importance of conservation and its relevance to the concerns of target groups.

To be more effective, conservationists need radically to change the public perception of their attitude to development. Too often conservationists have allowed themselves to be seen as resisting all development, although often they have been forced into that posture because they have not been invited to participate in the development process early enough. The result has been not to stop development, but to persuade many development practitioners, especially in developing countries, that conservation is not merely irrelevant but harmful and anti-social. Consequently, development has continued unimpeded by conservationists yet with the seeds of its eventual failure lying in the ecological damage that conservation could have helped to prevent.

Conservationists should work actively and positively for sustainable development. This does not mean that everything that calls itself development (whether sustainable or not) should be taken at face value. Many ill-conceived policies and projects will still need to be altered or scrapped altogether. But conservationists must come to distinguish more clearly and carefully between environmental alteration that is necessary and worth the biological cost and that which is not. Then they should work with development practitioners to ensure that development is indeed environmentally sound.

Several US conservation organizations have found that a more positive approach to development and its integration with conservation pays off. They have been able to alter the policies of the US Agency for International Development (AID), which annually spends some $1700 million in developing countries. The US NGOs have:

— ensured that AID makes environmental impact assessments before undertaking any environmentally significant activities;
— persuaded the Congress to add 'environment and natural resources' to the areas in which AID is statutorily required to spend its money;
— convinced the Congress to direct AID to prepare 'environmental profiles' of all the countries in which AID operates;
— persuaded the House of Representatives to make tropical forest protection a statutorily mandated priority for AID.

All these policy changes were brought about by US NGOs at a cost to them of $30,000.

The price of conservation, like that of freedom, is eternal vigilance. It is essential that conservationists follow through and consolidate their successes. This means monitoring. In the case of CITES, for example, conservation organizations should monitor the implementation of CITES by their national (scientific and management) authorities. They should monitor trading in shops and through newspaper and other advertisements. They should also ensure that the annual reports and any proposals submitted by national authorities to the CITES secretariat properly reflect conditions, informing the CITES secretariat should this not be the case. Conservation organizations with monitoring experience could provide a useful service to other organizations (especially in other countries or provinces) by helping them to set up their own monitoring systems.

What the individual can do

There are two kinds of action which the individual can take and which can help to speed and consolidate the Strategy's implementation. The first is to join a conservation organization and preferably one that is actively promoting (or intends to promote) the Strategy. In any case, the more living resource conservation organizations there are and the larger and more representative they are, the better.

For they will then be able to act more effectively and governments will be more likely to take notice of them.

The second kind of action, and one which may appeal more than the first to individuals in countries where non-governmental organizations are few or weak or where the political climate is unfavourable for them, is the alteration of personal behaviour. Change in personal habits of consumption was a much touted form of action in industrial countries during the late 1960s and early 1970s when environmentalism was fashionable. Since then it has fallen into disfavour, partly because it can seem so trivial but largely because it can involve real sacrifice. Few of the conservationists who inveigh against excessive energy consumption, for example, have abandoned their private cars for the admittedly erratic pleasure of public transport.

There is abundant evidence that all but the most punctilious conservationists will continue to fail to conserve the resources (whether living or non-living) they themselves use unless forced to do so by rises in price. Yet ultimately no conservation strategy or programme can succeed unless everyone actually *behaves* as a conservationist. Personal attempts to conserve resources may appear inconsequential in relation to the enormous problems addressed in this Strategy. At the same time they may involve apparently unjustified hardship for the individual. But such efforts are among the most significant of actions, the sum of which spread throughout society will mean real and enduring success.

Reference

1.Stein, Robert E and Johnson, Brian (1979) *Banking on the Biosphere: Environmental Procedures and Practices of Nine Multi-lateral Development Agencies* Lexiton Books